Dear Rowan....

Dear Rowan...

To the new Archbishop
of Canterbury, on saving
the Church of England
for the people of England.

John Hunt
Publishing Limited

Copyright © 2002 John Hunt Publishing Ltd

46A West Street, Alresford, Hants SO24 9AU, U.K.

Tel: +44 (0) 1962 736880 Fax: +44 (0) 1962 736881

E-mail: office@johnhunt-publishing.com

www.johnhunt-publishing.com

Text © 2002 Robert Van de Weyer

Designed by Nautilus Design, Basingstoke, Hants

ISBN 1 84298 098 X

A CIP catalogue record for this book is available from the British Library.

Printed in the U.K. by Ashford Colour Press

Contents

✠

Dear Rowan...

Dear Rowan...

✠

INTRODUCTION

I hope you will regard my writing this open letter as a sign of respect, rather than as an impertinence. As you said yourself when George Carey announced his retirement, the job of Archbishop of Canterbury makes impossible demands. Yet I believe it possible that you may perform the impossible.

In the mid- 1980s I made your acquaintance. At the time you were dean of a Cambridge college, and intent on protesting against the installation of Cruise nuclear missiles. I recall that you broke into the US base at Alconbury, and celebrated the Eucharist there. My wife and I had the more humdrum role of supplying logs to the protesters at Molesworth, where the missiles were to be sited – although I did baptize a baby who was born in one of the caravans there. I was aware from your writings, as well as from some discussion groups in which we both participated, that, while our political attitudes were closely allied, your theology was profoundly orthodox, while my theological views have always been heretical.

The nature of heresy – indeed, the root of the word itself – is freedom of thought; and in the intervening time I have moved even further from orthodoxy. The nature of orthodoxy is to remain unchanged. So I assume that my theological views have diverged even further from yours. Peter Walker, the saintly bishop who ordained me, seemed to relish my intellectual and spiritual roaming. He also welcomed my criticisms – wearing my professional hat as an economist – of the poor financial management of the Church; and in 1985 he even invited me to present a paper to him and his senior staff on the radical changes required to stave off perpetual financial crisis. But his suffragan, and then his successor, took a dimmer view; and they refused to renew my licence as non-stipendiary priest of the village of Upton. The people of Upton made clear at a public meeting and by letters that they still wanted me as their priest; and since I had committed no offence to justify my dismissal, I decided to continue ministering to them. Three years later I supported a group of parishes in west Norfolk when the bishop tried to foist a priest on them against their wishes. Thus, in the two decades since we met, I have gained the reputation as a turbulent priest. I have even been forbidden from preaching in four dioceses, and the *Church Times* has called for bme to be unfrocked for disobedience and fomenting schism.

My reputation may cause some to discount anything I say about the Church of England. But in the past the Church of England has had a place for rebels; and the rebels have generally been the source of fresh thinking. Whether or not they merit the epithet 'fresh', the thoughts presented in this letter are undoubtedly quite different from the prevailing attitudes within the Church of England. My claim on your attention is that, if fruits are some measure of rightness, these prevailing attitudes must to a great degree be wrong – and that new thinking is desperately needed. The fruits borne by the Church of England have become scanter and less sweet by the decade – and the statistics on church involvement compiled with such meticulous care by Dr Peter Brierley compel us even to contemplate the death of the tree itself over the next two or three generations. By contrast, my ideas, over a long period of twenty years, have been shown to work in Upton. Indeed, I make a further claim: that my ideas are firmly rooted in the traditions of the Church of England – they are radical in the proper sense of that overused word – while the prevailing attitudes are an aberration. And although my heretical convictions help to shape my ideas, they are also perfectly compatible with orthodoxy.

I write as a loyal rebel, who yearns to see the tree thrive.

Chapter 1

✚

TRUE AND FALSE PRIORITIES

Guarded optimism

When your predecessor, George Carey, was appointed archbishop twelve years ago, he was greeted with great optimism. The much-heralded Decade of Evangelism was just beginning, with the hope that by the turn of the millennium the long decline in church involvement might be reversed. And George Carey, whose ministry at St Nicholas Church, Durham a few years earlier had swelled its congregation, seemed ideally suited to lead an expansion of the entire Church of England. The early interviews after his appointment, despite a few minor slips, revealed a deep, unshakeable faith, and an easy, unthreatening manner – a combination that was attractive on television. And his choice of modern hymns at his enthronement indicated his commitment to ridding the Church of its dowdy image, and presenting it as fresh and lively. At the time of his appointment I was in northern Uganda; and a CMS missionary there, a young Englishman of strongly Evangelical convictions, was so delighted that he decided to offer himself for ordination.

Much as I admired – and still admire – George Carey, I did not share the optimism. I too am dedicated to reversing the decline in the Church of England; indeed, the primary purpose of this letter is to propose how this may be done. But the decline is not caused by poor presentation in the media, nor by old-fashioned hymns at our services. So improving our presentation and brightening our services will not help. While I do not begrudge George Carey's success in Durham, I know from friends in the city – and from my knowledge of similar success stories elsewhere – that the growth of St Nicholas was mainly at the expense of other churches, mostly non-Anglican, whose congregations dipped. The decline in the Church of England as a whole cannot be reversed by poaching from other denominations – and nor should it be. Our purpose must be to include those who currently are involved with no religious group.

Optimism of a somewhat different kind surrounds your appointment to Canterbury. You are rightly regarded as an intellectual heavyweight and Anglicans are proud at the prospect of being led by someone who can talk on equal terms with the finest brains in the land. And you are frequently described as holy. While I am wary of that adjective applied to any human being – we all have feet of clay – your integrity and wisdom are manifest; and that too causes pleasure to Anglicans. The obvious comparison, which many commentators have made, is with Basil Hume, the late Catholic archbishop. Like him, you carry great spiritual authority.

But the comparison with Cardinal Hume contains a warning. People always listened to him with respect, and many individual Christians were inspired by his words. Yet he was only occasionally heeded outside the confines of his Church – most notably in his interventions on cases of miscarriage of justice. And the decline in attendance at Mass accelerated during his tenure. So at his death the Catholic Church in England was significantly smaller and weaker than when he took charge. Certainly he improved the image of Catholicism amongst his compatriots, and this may have helped attract a few famous converts, such as Ann Widdecombe, John Gummer and Charles Moore, into his fold. But even the allegiance of the editor of the *Daily Telegraph* has done nothing to stem the exodus. When Cardinal Hume died, the writers of his obituaries recalled his diplomatic abilities, which protected English Catholicism from the reactionary excesses of the Vatican – and this, so they concluded, was his most solid achievement.

Perhaps it is unfair to have any expectations of a new Archbishop of Canterbury. The person filling this office has far less power over the Church than the Prime Minister has over the government. Tony Blair hires and fires all the ministers, and, through his party's majority in the House of Commons, largely determines what legislation is passed. The Archbishop of Canterbury by contrast has negligible power over the appointment of bishops and other senior clerics, and must work with whoever the arcane system throws up. And he has no party loyal to his bidding on the General Synod to vote for measures that meet his approval. To use the distinction coined by Walter Bagehot in regard to the British constitution, the Archbishop may be regarded as heading the 'dignified' part of the Church of England – though it is hard to see, by this analogy, who comprise the 'efficient' part.

But the analogy is misleading. The monarch, who heads the dignified part of the British constitution, is confined to uttering platitudes, and once a year at the opening of Parliament to being the mouthpiece of the government. Our present Queen performs this function superbly, managing to infuse her platitudes with grace and love, and even suggesting a weary scepticism at her government's proposals, but she has no tangible effect on the daily lives of her subjects. You, on the other hand, are expected to formulate and express your own ideas, and Anglicans are eager both to hear what you say, and to be influenced by it. In this respect you are even more powerful than a prime minister. The people of this country treat the words of their politicians with disdain but Anglicans give the words of their archbishop great weight.

The authority of the archbishop derives partly from the peculiar nature of religion. People tend to ascribe a special degree of divine inspiration to religious leaders and as a result, they tend to be more submissive to religious forms of authority than to secular forms. I regard this attitude as unhealthy, and in my parochial ministry go to considerable lengths to discourage it. As my father taught – and I have never found the source of this phrase: 'Bend the knee to no one, and let no one bend the knee to you.' But quite apart from this spiritual childishness, members of, and sympathizers with, the Church of England recognize that, at this particular juncture in its history, it desperately needs good leadership, and you are now in the best position to provide it.

Will your achievements be as meagre as those of your kindred spirit, Cardinal Hume? Or will your archepiscopate be the time when the graph of church involvement in this country at last changes direction? It depends on the way in which you seek to exert your influence.

The example of Tony Blair

Prime ministers are generally elected to office on promises to improve public services in the country – to make schools better at imparting knowledge, to make hospitals better at healing illnesses, and to make the roads and railways convey people more speedily from place to place. In the first flush of electoral success they believe that they can fulfil their promises, but after two or three years of hard slog, with scant signs of change, their attention gradually moves overseas. They relish the trips to summit conferences, where they can discuss with other leaders the great issues facing the world, and they enjoy making pompous pronouncements on global affairs. Tony Blair was entering this phase of his premiership before his second election victory, and his foreign forays seem to reassure him of his own importance. But while the people of Kosovo and Sierra Leone have reason to be grateful for his undoubted courage and moral zeal, most of his footsteps across the world leave no impression at all.

Archbishops of Canterbury also suffer the temptation of

phoney importance. Indeed, the temptation is even more acute, because of the hybrid nature of the office – the bishop of a diocese, the archbishop of a province, the senior archbishop in the Church of England, the focus of unity of the worldwide Anglican Communion, and also in some ill-defined way the moral and spiritual guardian of Great Britain.

The domestic problems of the Church of England are even more intractable than those in the National Health Service and the British transport system. There is, of course, the rapid and accelerating decline in attendance at church services; and this decline is most marked amongst the young, suggesting that the decline may accelerate further in the coming decades. Economic changes beyond its control, combined with its own incompetence, has reduced the amount that the Church Commissioners can pay towards clergy stipends and this has forced dioceses to ask for more and more from the laity. But despite large increases in the amount given by most lay people, the books still refuse to balance and, as congregations continue to fall, the total amount of lay contributions seems bound to fall as well. Until now the large number of clergy reaching retirement age has prevented any enforced redundancies, but unemployment amongst clergy, which has occurred in past eras, may soon haunt us again.

Although congregations were falling even in Victorian times, it is only since the early 1960s that the decline has become steep. During these past forty years there have been all kinds of innovations and initiatives to try and reverse it. There have been several new translations of the Bible, and two new service books; in addition, churches have experimented with various informal styles of worship. There have been numerous evangelistic missions, both nationally and locally. Synodical government has been introduced, making the Church democratic. Group and team ministries have been formed to encourage a more collaborative style of pastoral care; non-stipendiary ministers have become common; women priests are now very widely accepted and welcomed, and there have been numerous schemes to draw lay people into active ministry. Much good, and some excellent, work has been done and there seems little doubt that the quality of ministry in the Church of England is as good, and probably better, than it has ever been. But nothing has succeeded in stopping the rot. Even Alpha courses, currently hailed as the most effective form of evangelism, at best only reduce the rate of decline, and in many churches have no effect at all – as a survey commissioned by the Alpha organization itself revealed.

So why flog this stumbling horse? Why not do as Tony Blair and other prime ministers have done, and turn your attention to the wider international stage? Indeed, you do not even have to look to politics for an example to follow. George Carey soon became so engrossed in the wider Anglican Communion that some complained of his becoming invisible in England. Whereas here he was frequently written off as a mediocrity, in Africa and Asia he was cheered and embraced. Perhaps with children still at home you may be reluctant to embark on too many foreign trips. With your intellectual power there are plenty of other ways of lifting your eyes from the dismal parochial scene. You could concentrate on the ethical and ecclesiological issues that currently engross certain bishops and priests – such as homosexuality and women bishops. You could set about reformulating the link between the Church of England and the state to increase the Church's independence. You could even take a leaf out of Archbishop Fisher's book: he devoted much of his energy to revising English canon law; you are amply qualified to revise the Anglican doctrinal formulae.

All these possible activities would feel very important. But their importance is phoney, for the simple reason that the Church of England *is* its parishes; and unless these flourish, the rest is vanity and chasing the wind.

The example of Harold Wilson

In the early 1960s Harold Wilson was one of my heroes. I admired his apparent passion for justice, and his enthusiasm for modernization – 'the white heat of technology' sounded exciting to my adolescent mind. And I also appreciated his barded wit, which made him a hard target for the cast of *That Was The Week That Was*, who were also heroes. I had a transistor radio under my pillow in the school dormitory throughout that glorious night in October 1964 when Wilson won his first general election. But in the following six years, until he lost to Edward Heath in 1970, I, along with his numerous other admirers, watched with horror as he squandered his premiership. The main reason for his failure was that he turned inwards to his own party, struggling to prevent splits and to expose conspiracies. His method of maintaining party unity, as the political commentator Ian Aitkin put it, was to give sugar lumps alternately to the right-wing horses and the left-wing horses. Yet if he had concentrated on providing good and just government, the Labour Party would have united behind him without the need for sugar lumps.

For an Archbishop of Canterbury turning inwards means concentrating on the hierarchy of the Church, on the issues that excite it, and on the groups that compete for its attention. Large organizations of all kinds – commercial, as well as political and ecclesiastical – have a kind of inner dynamic that makes then try to capture and tame their leaders; and in the process the leaders are disabled. Harold Wilson, who through the 1940s and 1950s remained gloriously free and independent, allowed himself to be captured by the Labour Party after he became leader; and as a result he was a poor prime minister. In my view a similar fate befell George Carey, and to a lesser extent his predecessor Robert Runcie: the Church as an organization overwhelmed them, and so their vision became blurred and their energy was sapped. Michael Ramsey, by contrast, seemed to retain a high degree of detachment and he is remembered for the inspiration he gave both to churchgoers and to the entire nation.

Homosexuality is probably the greatest single issue that will tempt your attention inwards. In Britain as a whole it has almost ceased to raise pulse-rates; even the *Daily Mail* can congratulate the pop idol Will Young for declaring himself gay. And while anti-gay views probably remain more common within congregations, the issue is rarely discussed. Yet there is persistent talk of the Church splitting apart over homosexuality; even such an experienced bishop as Hugh Montefiore has smelt the aroma of schism. If you are not careful you could spend days, weeks, months and even years trying to maintain ecclesiastical unity. You could address the Lesbian and Gay Christian Movement, as I understand you intend to do, and throw them a few sugar lumps and then you could throw a few more lumps in the direction of Reform. You could chair commissions, draft reports, write articles, and speak at debates, until the whole business of sex became in your mind an arcane theological game.

But what would you have achieved? In the first place, regardless of what you had said, therey would not be one more, or one fewer, homosexual relationship in the world. Almost nobody would have changed their moral views on the subject and the church would be no more unified. On the contrary, the antagonists would be just as hostile to one another. Many years ago my wife and I were members of the Lesbian and Gay Christian Movement and in its membership list we were shown as the only heterosexuals. But, although we remain as positive as ever about homosexual partnerships, we resigned, because we see the fight to change the hierarchy's attitudes and rules as entirely fruitless. It is surely best, therefore, to find some means of declaring a truce, and then ignoring the matter. I have a hunch that those on both sides of the divide are grown-up enough to honour a truce, if you spell out honestly the consequences of continuing warfare – and then use your authority to beg for mutual charity. The same approach should be taken to any other moral and doctrinal issue on which the hierarchy, and the groups surrounding it, divide into factions.

You are not only a theologian of distinction, but also a prophet who is able to see the signs of the times, and respond to them. And a prophet by definition looks outwards. Your prophetic gift will serve this country well on the occasions – which, for maximum effect, should be quite rare – when you speak on some major national or international issue. It is most needed, however, in relation to the spiritual needs of ordinary people in our cities, towns and villages. The decline in church involvement is a measure of the appalling degree to which the Church of England is failing to meet those needs. The parish system is the means by which those needs have been met in the past, and is the primary means whereby the Church of England can meet them in the future. Let your prophetic gift be turned towards how our parishes may be reformed and renewed.

Chapter 2

✠

TRUE AND FALSE DECLINE

Getting worse more quickly

Throughout my adult lifetime – and yours – there have been optimists proclaiming that the decline in church involvement has 'bottomed out.' I can recall several such headlines in the *Church Times* during the thirty years I have subscribed to that publication. For me the epitome of this optimism is Richard Sledge, the retired Archdeacon of Huntingdon, a man of great warmth and gentleness with whom I have had some friendly skirmishes over the years. Shortly after his appointment – around 1982, I think – he came to dinner with my wife and me and our two young boys. I asked, intending to be provocative, how he felt about presiding over an archdeaconry where the prospect was continuing decline. He refused to be provoked, and answered calmly that the years of decline in the Church of England were now over, and we were entering a period of growth. About a decade later, when he was preaching at the annual service for churchwardens, he declared roundly that ... the years of decline in the Church of England were now over, and we were entering a period of growth. In the intervening years congregations had fallen by over a fifth.

My experience is that most senior clergy are like spiritual estate agents. They are always talking up the market, even when the indicators point firmly down. And when they turn their eyes to a particular parish, well, a little bit of modernization here, and some modest improvements there, and the punters will soon be flocking. Perhaps sunny optimism is part of the job of being a senior cleric. After all, if estate agents told prospective buyers that prices were falling, they would make no sales.

One day the optimists may be right. Religious organizations can get down to a hard core of people for whom the organization is perfectly suited. But in the process the organization gets narrower and more homogeneous, as the hard core of members adapt it to their requirements. Indeed, as I shall explore, the Church of England is showing ominous signs of narrowing, which is hastening its present decline, but may eventually halt the decline when only the hard core remains. The optimists may be proved right even earlier, if the country suffers some military, economic, political or environmental crisis. There was a brief upward blip in church attendance after the World Trade Center terrorist attack: although it occurred across the Atlantic, the attack felt close. Similar attacks on our own soil would presumably have a greater effect on church attendance although that seems a high price to pay for filling our pews.

At present, however, the optimists seem horribly wrong. When sales at Marks and Spencers fell by a few percentage points for three or four years in a row in the late 1990s, it was regarded as a catastrophe for the company, and its shares plummeted; a new chief executive was appointed, and he promised to reverse the slide in sales within eighteen months. The problem for the Church of England is far, far worse than that faced by M&S. During both the 1980s and the 1990s Sunday attendance fell by just under a quarter: the cumulative loss over the two decades was just over 40 per cent. So if a church had, say, a normal congregation of 50 in 1980, it typically had around 30 in 2000. Of course, the situation is far from uniform: many churches declined by more, while some churches actually increased and I want to explore those variations in more detail later. But the overall picture could hardly be worse.

Actually, it is worse. In the first place, the loss during the 1980s and 1990s was probably even greater than that in the previous two decades – although figures are much less reliable during the earlier period. So that undermines any easy talk about bottoming out. Secondly, and more ominously, the loss was much greater amongst the young, and much less amongst the elderly and this trend is accelerating. According to Peter Brierley's survey, over the past two decades the number of children and teenagers attending church has halved, and most of that decline was in the 1990s. The number of people in their twenties attending church has almost halved. And the number in their thirties and forties dropped in the 1980s by 7 per cent, and in the 1990s by 20 per cent- almost three times as much. The fact that numbers over sixty-five dropped by only 5 per cent over the two decades is partly explained by people living longer, although a more robust commitment amongst the elderly has also helped.

To my knowledge there are no statistical analyses of the

lifetime pattern of individual churchgoers. But all of us involved in parish life have met many people who attended church as children, often as part of a Sunday school; they dropped away in the busy years of young adulthood then at around the age of fifty, as the nest emptied, they resumed attending. That pattern was even observed in medieval times, and is the reason why church congregations have always been dominated by the old and the young. My wife and I also observed it in the Orthodox Church of Ethiopia, where we lived in the early 1970s. But now that children are deserting the Church of England, will they attend when they reach middle age? I fear not. They will not have that deep-rooted familiarity with the culture of the Church that former generations acquired in childhood and so the Church will feel strange and alien – and therefore unattractive. Indeed, as someone who converted from anti-Christian hostility to Christianity at the age of twenty, I know just how peculiar the Church feels to someone who was not raised in it; I felt I was entering a foreign country.

Peter Cook once parodied Harold Macmillan's efforts to convince us that we had never had it so good: 'I am pleased to announce that the British economy is getting worse more slowly.' We cannot even say that about the Church of England; it is getting worse more quickly.

From three parties to one

After I became a Christian in 1970, I spent three years floating between denominations. That was easy and convenient, since my partner (who soon became my wife) and I were travelling during much of that period. Being a bookworm, I also studied in detail the history and doctrines of each denomination, even reading the entire outpourings of both the First and the Second Vatican Councils of the Roman Catholic Church – a feat that possibly deserves a mention in the Guinness Book of Records.

I was attracted by the internationalism of the Catholic Church, exemplified by its various Uniat churches in Asia which use the traditional local liturgies and I frequently attended Mass. But I found myself unable to accept the Catholic concept of the priest as mediator between God and human beings; nor could I accept its claim to be the sole true church. At the other end of the spectrum I was also attracted to the liberalism and pacifism of the Quakers but religion for me, as for most people, requires symbols and rituals, which Quakers reject. I was never drawn to any form of Evangelicalism, repelled by its doctrinal narrowness and – so it seems to me – shallow emotionalism. Indeed, having become a Christian via Hinduism and Jainism, I could never embrace any form of Christianity that rejected all other religions as wrong. When we lived in Ethiopia, I fell in love with the Orthodox Church of that country, especially its monasteries which we were studying. I admired its deep historical roots, and was pleased that it makes no special claims, regarding itself merely as being the church of a particular nation. But, of course, it is not my nation.

I joined the Church of England in 1973 when we settled in Lancaster, where we spent four years. I was confirmed in the following March alongside a large and noisy cohort of adolescent boys and girls. Confirmation, in those far-off days, was still the conventional 'rite of passage' for young teenagers. The boys, I recall, were instructed to use water on their hair, instead of Brylcream, on the day of the service to prevent the bishop's hands from transferring Brylcream onto the girls' newly-permed heads. My reasons for seeking confirmation within the Church of England were the mirror image of my reasons for not asking to join the Ethiopian Orthodox Church. The Church of England has deep historical roots, and yet makes no special claims about itself except that it belongs to a particular nation – my own. Despite my Flemish name, I am irredeemably English and I wanted to belong to an English church. Three weeks after my confirmation at Christ Church, Lancaster, I was elected churchwarden of the parish – an office that I have come to regard as the most important in the Church of England.

England has been a famously tolerant country and this tolerance has been embodied in the Church of England's ability to hold together people of very different theological convictions and tastes in worship. The historians of the Church of England typically speak if its genius for being 'comprehensive', and describe three parties within it. First, there is the High Church party, which in their older form were known as Laudians, after your seventeenth-century predecessor Archbishop Laud, and then transmogrified in the nineteenth century into Tractarians and Anglo-Catholics. They emphasize the place of Anglicanism within the universal church, and tend to like Catholic-style ritual. This, I think, is the party with which you most closely identify. Secondly, there is the Low Church party, which began as the Puritans, but then, after some arguments over predestination in the eighteenth century, became the Evangelicals. They tend to emphasize the importance of personal conversion. Thirdly, there is the Broad Church party, whose intellectual ancestors in the seventeenth century were known as Latitudinarians, and who today are more commonly known as liberals. They sit lightly on doctrinal formulae, embrace scientific ways of thinking, and are open to insights from other religions.

To a novice Anglican in Lancaster in the early 1970s, these three parties were not simply figments of history, but were readily visible. The Priory church was liberal, although socially rather stuffy, and so was St Chad's. St Luke's was moderately Evangelical, while St Thomas's was rampantly so and Christ Church was unashamedly Anglo-Catholic, with the vicar being called 'Father'. From the outset I was strongly liberal. But Christ Church happened to be our parish church, and Father Salman and the congregation welcomed us warmly so we felt perfectly comfortable there.

But during the past three decades the three party system has been rapidly disappearing, and it will soon be extinct.

According to Peter Brierley's statistics, the number of Anglican churches described by their clergy as 'liberal' fell by a quarter during the 1990s, while those described by their clergy as 'evangelical' rose by a quarter. At the same time attendance at 'liberal' churches fell sharply, while 'evangelical' churches held their own. The statistics in his earlier book describing the 1980s are compiled rather differently, so direct comparisons are difficult but these trends were clearly marked during that decade also. During both decades the position of Anglican churches described by their clergy as 'catholic' has become worse than that of the evangelical churches, but better than that of the liberals.

Although these statistics are striking, in my view they greatly underestimate the enormity of what has occurred. The clergy in general have become doctrinally stricter and more orthodox, and more assertive of the distinctiveness of the Christian system of beliefs and 'world-view', as against other systems and views. This is an understandable response to the marginal position in which Christianity now finds itself within Britain; minority groups are always prone to emphasize their differences from the majority. The result is that the whole spectrum of churchmanship has shifted several points away from liberalism towards orthodoxy – just as the spectrum of British politics has shifted several points to the right over the past two decades. Thus the liberal position held by clergy like me is an awkward relic from the past, like Old Labour. In regard to Peter Brierley's statistics,

I suspect that most churches described by their clergy as 'liberal' are a good deal less liberal in their doctrinal stance than they were in the past and 'evangelical' churches are doctrinally even stricter.

A similar shift has occurred amongst the laity. Just as my wife and I, despite being liberals, happily attended an Anglo-Catholic church in the 1970s, so churches of all descriptions had a large contingent of liberals within their congregations – for the simple reason that in the past most Anglican lay people were liberal-minded. The decline in church-going since the 1970s has, I strongly believe, been overwhelmingly amongst liberals. Thus not only have churches described as 'liberal' suffered, but also the decline in other churches has been largely due to the loss of liberals in their congregations. It is not hard to see why this should be so. Liberals may be deeply religious, as I am, but tend to be less committed to organized religion. As the clergy have become doctrinally stricter, the liberals, instead of staying to register dissent, have preferred to vote with their feet and a new generation of liberals sympathetic to Christianity have not joined. And as the pressure of other attractions and commitments has increased over recent decades, so liberals have been the first to chop church-going – or not take it up.

There has also been a minor intellectual crisis for liberals. In the past liberal Christians, while acknowledging the wisdom of other religions, blithely assumed that Christianity is in general superior. In our multi-cultural and multi-media society, greater awareness of other religions has made this attitude seem arrogant and patronizing. Many liberals have concluded that the only honest positions are to compete enthusiastically in the religious market place against the other religions, as full-blooded Evangelicals do, or to treat all religions with equal respect – and so affiliate with none. Liberals have typically chosen the latter option.

As the process of liberal retreat has continued, the position for the remaining liberals has become more and more difficult – and so the process has acquired a growing momentum. This momentum is enhanced by the way in which members of any group tend to reinforce one another's beliefs and opinions. Religious conversations amongst Anglicans, both informal ones after services and formal ones at discussion groups, tend now to assume a far greater degree of orthodox belief than they did when I first joined the Church of England. And, of course, in this context the clergy feel an even greater impulsion to preach orthodoxy.

One might have expected that, as the Broad Church party disappeared, the two remaining parties, Low and High, would have become more distinct from one another, and perhaps more antagonistic. But in fact the opposite has happened. Evangelicals and Anglo-Catholics have tended to emphasize their similarities to one another and it has become quite fashionable for bishops and clergy to describe themselves as 'Evangelical Catholics' or 'Catholic Evangelicals.' This merging of identities is presumably bound up with the growing sense of Christians being a minority in society; different groups within the minority naturally grow closer. The effect is that a single form of Anglicanism is rapidly emerging, with only minor variations within it. Its major doctrinal convictions conform to the pronouncements of the great councils of the first millennium – Nicea, Ephesus and Chalcedon – and so are the same as those of the Roman Catholic and most of the Orthodox churches, but there is an added Evangelical emphasis on personal commitment. Its style of worship tends to favour Evangelical hymnody, both new and old, yet also stresses the centrality of the Eucharist.

This reduction of parties from three to one has the consequence of reducing greatly the divisive squabbles in the Church of England. Indeed, I regard the pressure to soften the Church's stance on homosexuality as the last spasm of liberalism. But while this will reduce the demands on you to fight doctrinal and ethical fires amongst your senior colleagues, it makes the task of reversing the Church's decline far harder – a homogeneous church by its nature only attracts one kind of person. In my mind this homogeneity is symbolized by the new Church of England logo, a clever combination of the letters C and E, with a cross in the middle incorporating the middle arm of the E – usually printed or sewn onto a purple background. To put it rather crudely, and with a little hyperbole, the Church of England is ceasing to be comprehensive, and becoming a religious brand.

Exploring without belonging

For the past few years my village of Upton has participated in the Open Gardens scheme in which one afternoon in summer the general public is invited to visit the gardens of our most eager gardeners. We also open the church, which is bog-standard English gothic, and put a few more flower displays than normal on its ledges and tables. My impression is that most of the visitors to the gardens also pop into the church, and wander round for a few minutes and I enjoy observing them. They are not, with one or two exceptions, architectural buffs, busily pointing to bosses and capitals. As they move round the church, their bodies and faces relax, and their movements become slower and calmer and, if they talk to one another, their voices are low and respectful. They are attracted by, and are responding to, the spirit that an ancient church symbolizes, and which seems to permeate its fabric.

This is a manifestation of an astonishing religious phenomenon of our time, which church statistics like Peter Brierley's never record: that probably more people than ever before come to church – but avoid the times when services are being held. The numbers crossing the thresholds of our great cathedrals, and our major churches such as those at Boston and Tewkesbury, are vast and even quite ordinary parish churches have a steady trickle, as a glance at their visitors' books reveals. So, as our Sunday congregations dwindle, church-going has become one of

England's most popular activities. My two sons, now in their mid-twenties, are typical: they are allergic to typical Anglican religion; but wherever they go, they like to nip into the local church. Of course, they have a childhood background of visiting churches, but their friends mostly do the same.

On the millennium eve Upton witnessed another religious sign of our times. A few months earlier I had written an article in the village newssheet, inviting suggestions for ways of marking the millennium in the church. The chairman of the church council, Richard Sandilands, suggested commissioning a new collection plate, with the symbols of the main religions of the world on its rim – representing our hope that the third millennium would be an era of religious peace. So a local artist produced a wooden plate, with the symbols of Taoism, Hinduism, Buddhism, Judaism, Islam and Christianity carved in relief. And we held a service dedicating the plate, with readings from the various religions. Comparatively few people from Upton itself came, as they were revelling elsewhere – although everyone subsequently showed great appreciation of the plate. But a surprisingly large number of young people from outside the village turned up. They were not, of course, regular churchgoers, but they were encouraged and delighted that a particular church was celebrating global religious unity.

Back in the late 1960s, when I took the overland route to

India, I was part of an elite of privileged young men and women, mostly educated in private schools and financed by inherited wealth, who experimented with oriental religions as we consciously rejected Christianity, which we regarded as narrow and hypocritical. Today, thirty-five years later, people of all ages take for granted that all religions, including Christianity, contain wisdom and many young people are quite eager to acquire religious wisdom, from any and every source, to help them in their passage through life. Paradoxically, although far fewer people attend services, Christianity is treated with respect by a far greater number of people – along with all the other religions.

Grace Davie, the sociologist of religion, has described modern religiosity in Britain as 'believing without belonging.' I am rather sceptical about the opinion polls, quoted by Grace Davie, that suggest belief in God remains widespread, and my scepticism is affirmed by the Adult Spirituality Project conducted by David Hay and Kate Hunt. They refer to the widespread belief in 'something there' and in some kind of 'universal consciousness' – which is a long way from the personal, Trinitarian God proclaimed by orthodox Christianity. Most people are agnostic, in the sense in which many years ago the great Methodist preacher, Leslie Weatherhead, referred to 'Christian agnosticism': they recognize that they know very little about what lies beyond their own perception. Yet nonetheless they are religious, in the sense that they are exploring ways of deepening and enriching their inner, spiritual experience; in Hay and Hunt's term, most people see religion as a 'quest'. So modern religiosity in Britain is perhaps better characterized as 'exploring without belonging'.

It is no exaggeration, in my view, to say that Britain is in the midst of a religious revival – or perhaps at the beginning of a huge religious revival. Although liberals like me have become an endangered species within the Church of England, liberal religion is flourishing as never before.

I fear that many of the Evangelical Catholics and Catholic Evangelicals now dominating the Church of England are glad to be rid of the liberals, whom they tend to regard as subversive. And, as I shall describe in the next chapter, they have enacted over recent decades various quite specific changes in the practices of the Church of England that have in effect excluded liberals. Equally it is tempting for liberals to conclude that, so long as religion in general is thriving, it hardly matters what happens to the Church of England in particular. Any liberal today having dealings with the Church of England is liable quite quickly to say, 'Bugger the lot of them.' But I have spent the past twenty years in Upton resisting and reversing the changes in the Church of England, and making a few changes of my own, in order to include the ordinary liberal-minded people of the parish; and I have enjoyed far greater success than I could have anticipated. In later chapters I shall try to explain how the Church of England as a whole may seek once again to embrace the liberals – and why it should do so.

Dear Rowan...

Chapter 3

✠

HARDENING THE EDGES

Raising the price

In an edition of *Crockford's Clerical Directory*, published eighty years' ago, the anonymous writer of the Preface chided clergy for paying the parish quota out of their own pockets. Lay people, the writer declared, should take financial responsibility for the Church on which the salvation of their souls depended.

The quota had been introduced as the golden financial summer of the Church of England turned into a chilly autumn. The agricultural boom of the mid-nineteenth century had hugely increased the Church's income both from rents and from tithes. Parishes paid their vicar's stipend from their own resources; and under Queen Victoria virtually every parish could afford to pay a vicar an adequate stipend, with many parishes providing very handsome stipends. As a result almost every parish had its own resident priest; and most of the priests built themselves very large vicarages, employing several servants to cook, clean, mow the lawns, and tend the horses. Many priests even had surplus money with which to build schools. The priest in Upton built himself a quite hideous mansion, in a peculiar mixture of crude gothic and even cruder Georgian, with an admixture of Tudor; he also erected a brick shed to serve as a school room, on the site opposite the church where my wife and I have built our home – in a Flemish style.

But the agricultural depression, which began in the late Victorian period, and continued with occasional respite until the late 1950s, destroyed much of the Church's wealth. Then, just before the depression ended, the Church sold most of its agricultural land, and shifted into financial assets. So it largely missed out on the huge boom in agricultural land prices and rents of the 1960s and 1970s, during which they rose forty-fold, and while its shares rose in value about tenfold in the same period, its investment in fixed interest bonds of various kinds languished. Then, of course, it lost the best part of £1 billion – estimates of the exact amount vary – in the recession of the late 1980s and early 1990s, through a quite lunatic piece of financial speculation. Thus the vast mountain of ecclesiastical wealth has eroded to a modest outcrop.

In the first decade of the twentieth century many clergy found themselves reduced to a form of genteel poverty which was more uncomfortable than actual poverty: they continued to live in vast vicarages, without enough money for servants to clean them or for fuel to heat them. At the end of the First World War the gradual process of amalgamating rural parishes began, in an effort to boost the incomes of the clergy that remained. Upton lost its resident priest in 1919, and the hideous mansion was sold; initially the parish was joined with one other parish, then two, then five – and then I arrived as its unpaid priest. And in the meantime a higher and higher proportion of the clergy stipends had to be financed by the direct giving of the laity.

Now we have at last reached the point where for all

practical purposes the laity must finance the whole cost of the parochial ministry, while the inherited wealth of the Church covers most of the central costs. That *Crockford's* writer would presumably approve. So too would Mahatma Gandhi. He enunciated the principle that voluntary organizations of all kinds should deliberately avoid accumulating wealth, and should depend wholly on direct giving; only by this means will they remain accountable to the public that they are seeking to serve. I entirely agree, and regard the incompetence of the Church Commissioners, who have been stewards of most of the Church's wealth, as potentially a great blessing.

But changes in the administrative structure of the Church have turned the blessing into a curse. If parishes had been allowed to remain financially independent, as they had been since their formation in Saxon times, then we should have the accountability that Gandhi advocated. Large parishes would be free to decide the number of clergy they wished to maintain; and small rural parishes would decide how to share clergy – or alternatively develop voluntary forms of ministry. Equally the paid clergy would answer to their parishes as to how they used their time. Such a system may seem at first sight rather daunting, especially for the clergy themselves,; and it has dangers, which I shall discuss later. But, not only is it spiritually beneficial for the laity, as the *Crockford's* writer implied, but the clergy's position would be no different from that of people in the commercial world

- if you run a coffee shop in the high street, you are answerable to your customers.

Yet, as the Church's wealth has diminished, so it has centralized its financial administration. Until 1948 the Church had two central funds from which it topped up the income of poor parishes. But now all the remaining wealth of the Church is held centrally by the Church Commissioners and by the individual dioceses. At the same time the quota imposed on parishes – now given the euphemism 'parish share' – has to cover clergy stipends and pension contributions. And since power always follows money, the diocesan authorities decide how many clergy to employ, and where to deploy them. This system of diocesan control has become so firmly established that people have forgotten how new it is: it dates mainly from the end of the Second World War, and in its full form is less than three decades old.

Defenders of the system claim that accountability is achieved by means of democracy, since a diocese's budget must be approved by the diocesan synod. But such accountability is largely illusory. In the first place, mass democracy is a very blunt instrument of accountability; the NHS is far less accountable to patients, even though it is ultimately controlled by an elected parliament, than is an osteopath who charges patients £25 a session. Secondly, the diocesan synod is not elected by the church members, but is elected by the members of deanery synods, so the lines of accountability are indirect. Thirdly, in practice the details of a diocesan budget are decided long before they reach the diocesan synod, so ordinary synod members have very little control. And fourthly, the synod has no power whatever over clergy deployment, which in theory is decided jointly by the bishop and local patrons, but in practice is largely determined by the bishop in consultation with the archdeacons.

Thirty years ago, as the quota began seriously to impinge on parish finances, there was a fashion for 'stewardship campaigns', which in my experience always included a 'stewardship supper' consisting of shepherd's pie and peas. There was much talk of the stewardship of abilities as well as money; but the real purpose was to raise weekly donations. More recently, bishops and senior clerics have resorted to direct appeals, and churchgoers have been asked to give 5 per cent of their post-tax income to the Church; and sometimes these appeals are combined with vague threats to close down churches that fail to meet their quota. Not uncommonly giving to the Church is equated with 'giving to God'.

Any student of business economics knows that centralized systems of financial control lead to all kinds of inefficiencies. But, while this is undoubtedly true of the Church of England, the main problem of centralization is that it distorts the entire ministry and mission of the local parish. To join a parish church nowadays is to put yourself under great moral pressure both to dig deeply into your own pocket, and to involve yourself in a ceaseless round of fund-raising activities. If you feel that your charitable giving is better directed at Oxfam or Save the Children, or if you dislike fetes and jumble sales, then you had better keep clear. Moreover, it has become much more difficult to have only an occasional involvement with the local church; as soon as you show your face, the hard-pressed existing members start begging your help. Church involvement thus carries a very high price in both money and time – or else in guilt. The late John Robinson, who became famous as the Bishop of Woolwich who in 1963 wrote *Honest to God*, spoke approvingly of the 'soft edges' of the Church of England. The present financial system has greatly hardened them.

For the past ten or fifteen years the centralized financial system has been tottering, especially in some rural dioceses. Generous subsidies from English Heritage for church repairs haves helped to maintain the system, by enabling parishes to divert an increasing proportion of their funds to the quota. And affluent people from cities who have bought houses in villages, but rarely attend services, have also been willing to contribute large sums for church repairs – enabling an even higher proportion of the weekly collection to go towards the quota. In addition dioceses have staved off bankruptcy by having longer gaps between vicars, thereby reducing the actual cost of clergy stipends without further major reductions in the number of clergy posts – a somewhat dishonest wheeze, although politically shrewd. But as the number of people attending services continues to drop, and as the average age of worshippers rises, so the system must eventually collapse. And the collapse, when it comes, could be quite rapid. As a significant number of parishes fail to meet their full quota, the quota on the other parishes must rise to make up the shortfall – and this will increase the number of defaulters, leading to further rises.

Anti-reform Acts

From the first Reform Act of 1832, there was a series of Reform Acts through the nineteenth and early twentieth centuries that progressively widened the political franchise, until all sane men and women were entitled to vote in local and national elections. In the Church of England the opposite has occurred: since the Parochial Church Councils Measure of 1921 the ecclesiastical franchise has progressively and drastically narrowed.

The Church of England was the pioneer of democracy. The office of churchwarden was the first democratically elected office in the country, dating back at least to the thirteenth century. As far as historians can discern, every male in a parish was entitled from that time both to vote for the churchwardens and to stand as a churchwarden. Indeed, the principle of democracy was so ruthlessly applied that a man could be nominated without his consent; and if elected, he was compelled by law to serve. From the late nineteenth century onwards a number of parishes began to experiment with having church councils that shared some of the churchwardens' responsibilities. This appeared to be an extension of democracy, in the sense that a council of several members can represent a greater range of opinion than the normal complement of two churchwardens. But in most parishes restrictions were put on those who could both elect and serve on parochial church councils, to ensure that they were in some way committed to the Christian faith – or, more precisely, to the form of the faith espoused by the clergy and senior laity in the parish. Not surprisingly, parochial church councils were most popular in urban parishes that were Anglo-Catholic or Evangelical; more liberal parishes were content with the old system.

The parochial church council (PCC) was brought within the orbit of ecclesiastical law in 1921; and although parishes were not required by law to have one, they soon became normal. The law relating to PCCs was further tightened in a measure in 1956, which stipulated clearly their responsibilities; these essentially involve managing the material assets of the church, and cooperating with the priest in 'promoting the whole mission of the church, pastoral, evangelistic, social and ecumenical' – responsibilities that for the previous seven centuries churchwardens had carried. Then the Synodical Government Measure of 1969 laid down precise rules for the conduct of elections. The nub of these rules is that only those who are baptized, and who declare themselves in writing to be 'members' of the Church of England (or belong to a denomination in 'communion' with it), are allowed to join the roll of people that elects the PCC; and only communicants can be elected. This breaches one of the basic rules of democracy, that the electors and those eligible for election should be one and the same body of people. More importantly, it restricts the lay management of the parish church to a tiny segment of the people living in the parish – in most cases to no more than 5 per cent of the adults, and in many cases to barely 2 per cent.

The roles that remain specific to churchwardens are now quite limited. Yet they are *ex officio* members of their PCC, and generally regarded as the leading members of it. So they often function as both initiators of topics for discussion, and executors of decisions made. They have also historically been the foci of resistance to priestly or episcopal innovations. In the seventeenth century there were several famous court cases between churchwardens and vicars, in which churchwardens challenged the rights of vicars to change styles of worship, and to re-order church furniture accordingly. The courts generally found in favour of the churchwardens. In recent decades churchwardens in rural parishes have often led opposition to pastoral schemes proposed by bishops to amalgamate more and more parishes under a single priest.

The rules for electing churchwardens have become extremely messy, as there has been a commendable opposition to change amongst those who cherish the Church's democratic traditions – and this has led to awkward compromises. It remains the case that every adult resident living in the parish, whose name appears on the local government register of electors, is entitled to vote for the churchwardens; in addition those on the church electoral roll as regular worshippers, but not resident in the parish, are allowed to vote. In general churchwardens should be on the church electoral roll, and should be communicants, but the bishop is allowed to waive this requirement. Thus, with episcopal blessing the old system could still operate: the churchwarden could be anyone in the parish, chosen by everyone in the parish. But in general the restrictions applying to PCCs also apply to churchwardens.

These rules date from 1964. A new Churchwardens Measure was proposed in the late 1990s which would have given bishops power to sack churchwardens, without having to give reasons, and without possibility of appeal. The first meeting of the campaign against this innovation was in Upton, although people elsewhere – mainly in Norfolk – did the hard work of lobbying the Ecclesiastical Committee of Parliament. Bishops and other senior figures in the General Synod gave all kinds of assurances that this power would only be used in exceptional circumstances – such as the discovery that a churchwarden was a paedophile. But inevitably opponents were suspicious that bishops would get rid of churchwardens opposing their pastoral schemes. And

Parliament was also unconvinced, arguing that the secular law was the right means of dealing with criminals, and that parishioners themselves were in the best position to judge and reject those who were unsuitable for other reasons. The eventual Measure was little different from the 1964 legislation. It does, however, require churchwardens, before being admitted to office, to appear before the bishop or the bishop's 'substitute', and declare that they 'will faithfully and diligently' perform their duties. So the bishops gained a little symbolic power, but no extra actual power.

The most notable consequence of these restrictions on democracy has been in people's attitudes to church buildings. When Pope Gregory in the sixth century sent Augustine on his great mission to England, he instructed him – according to Bede's account – to treat the pagan places of worship with respect; instead of destroying them, he should seek to turn them into Christian places of worship. Gregory understood that the place of worship in a community is the main focus of popular religiosity, and thence an important means through which people's spiritual attitudes can be changed and transformed. He also understood that people feel a sense of ownership towards these buildings, and so the destruction of them would be felt as a severe personal affront. Churches remain a major focus of religiosity; the window above my desk looks across to Upton church, and I frequently observe people lingering in the churchyard, enjoying their proximity to the church. The huge number visiting cathedrals and churches is an index of their continuing spiritual importance for the British population as a whole. But people no longer feel that their parish church belongs to them; instead it belongs to the 'pious lot' who have signed up as members. They sense an invisible barrier that in some degree alienates them from the building, and thence from what it symbolizes.

The spirit behind the legislative changes of the past century is undoubtedly a rejection of the missionary theology of Pope Gregory. That enlightened pontiff wanted to keep the edges soft between paganism and Christianity, because he saw paganism not as the enemy of Christianity, but as a path towards to it. Many clergy today, however, are suspicious of what they habitually call 'folk religion', and fear that it taints the true faith. Thus the law has been re-framed to exclude all folk religionists from the Church's counsels.

Ministry as human resource management

When in 1977 I was preparing for a selection conference in Chester, to determine whether I was suitable for ordination, friends joked that success was a foregone conclusion: I have a posh accent, I was educated at a major public school, and I am the third son of a family mentioned in *Debrett's Peerage*. In those days, a quarter of a century ago, people still regarded the Church of England as the 'Tory Party at prayer'; and I was the epitome of the kind of man the Church liked to ordain. In the intervening years the Tory Party has changed hugely; indeed, a leading light in the Huntingdon Conservative Association said to me recently – only half in jest – that, were I to join, my poshness would debar me from gaining even minor office. The Church of England has also changed, and was already changing in the late 1970s. I do not think it has fallen victim to inverted snobbery, but to its credit it has become virtually indifferent to social background. Instead, judging by those being ordained, and by what people within the system have told me, I have the impression that that the selectors look for two key qualities in future priests: their personal faith should be sound; and they should be good and efficient managers of people. I would now be rejected on both grounds.

The requirement for sound faith is part of the shift towards orthodoxy. The requirement for efficient managers of people is to some degree a symptom of the Church's tendency to pick up ideas from business theory – but a decade or two after business theorists themselves have abandoned them. Back in the 1970 and 1980s, when Japan and Germany were the two most successful economies, theorists concluded that their secret was the way managers closely monitored their workers. Workers were regarded as 'human resources', and the managers' task was to monitor these resources so they performed to the maximum advantage. This approach was especially suitable for large corporations, where there was a perpetual danger of workers slacking; and largeness was seen as essential for efficiency. The favoured term was 'total quality management' – TQM – and the Church of England has become a leading practitioner.

The attractions of TQM to the Church of England are obvious. Although the numbers attending services have fallen, the typical modern vicar has charge of a far larger and more complex organization than his predecessor had two or three generations ago. Rural priests have several church buildings whose gutters need clearing and towers re-pointing; they chair several PCCs, working out a separate agenda for each; and they have to juggle several routines of worship. Urban parishes have doubled and tripled in population since Victorian times, while the number of assistant curates has plummeted; and people still look to the Anglican parson to conduct funerals and – to a diminishing extent – weddings. As the demands on the priests' time have increased, so priests have had to devolve more and more of their responsibilities onto lay people. But since lay people receive no money for their work, priests must ensure that every task devolved to them brings its own intrinsic rewards. So the successful priest, as the only paid professional in a voluntary organization, must learn to manage people with exceptional skill.

The notion of priest as person-manager is frequently given theological justification with reference to Paul's various lists of spiritual gifts: the priest is seen as drawing out and coordinating the gifts of the laity – he or she is the 'enabler'.

But beneath this happy, and apparently rational, fusion of theology and business theory there is madness. I frequently ask priests how they spend their time. Most have difficulty in answering, because they cannot immediately recall all the different tasks they perform in the course of a week. From the confused replies that I eventually receive, I estimate that they typically spend around a third of their time in raising money, and another large chunk in enabling others to raise money – which includes attending innumerable meetings when fund-raising events are planned. And most of this money now goes to meeting the quota – which in turn is used for paying the priest's salary. Thus in practice modern priests spend the greater part of their working hours chasing their own tails. Another substantial part, of course, is spent at deanery and diocesan meetings – which many clergy regard as chasing one another's tails.

The biggest casualty of this tail-chasing is general visiting within the parish. In my brief training for the priesthood I was taught that general visiting was an inefficient allocation of a priest's time. Modern priests should be in close personal touch only with the members of their own congregations – and they should encourage and train their members to make contact with their neighbours. In practice this advice is superfluous, since priests today have no time to reach beyond their congregations, except when a family has requested a funeral or a wedding. Thus priests have in their head a very clear picture of their sheepfold, and of the sheep grazing within it, and these sheep are the objects of their ministry. But the sheep outside the fold are a blur. Insofar as the sheep outside the fold ever think about the Church, they are aware of their status in the vicar's mind. And they express with surprising frequency some mild resentment, often using identical words: 'We never see the vicar nowadays.'

The busy community

In 1945 the Church of England produced a report with the grand title *Towards the Conversion of England*. The main authors were two bishops of Evangelical persuasion; and they defined the aim of evangelism as 'so to present Jesus Christ in the power of the Holy Spirit, that men shall come to put their trust in God through him, to accept him as their saviour, and serve him as their king in the fellowship of his church.' This form of words, and the theology underlying it, derives in large measure from John Wesley, who through his rejection of the Calvinist Puritanism of such contemporaries as Augustus Toplady and George Whitefield, and through the intensity of his own conversion, redefined the Christian mission. For him being a Christian was to make a personal commitment to Jesus Christ, and then to gather frequently with other people who had made a similar commitment. To enable converts to gather, he founded numerous local Methodist societies, and with their class meetings, lectures, and committees, these societies absorbed most of the leisure hours of their members. Thus to be a Christian was, under Wesley's tutelage, to be extremely busy; and the two Evangelical bishops dreamt of the Church of England teeming with busy Christians.

The report received a mixed reception. The Anglo-Catholics still held a strong position, and they saw the Christian mission rather differently. They believed in the objective spiritual power of the sacraments; and to be a Christian was to participate in the sacramental life of the Church. Most Anglo-Catholics were suspicious of sudden personal conversions, and preferred to see people attain holiness gradually through regular attendance at Communion. Their own vision for the post-war era was expressed through the Parish and People movement, formed in 1949, which sought to replace 'sung Matins' with 'sung Communion' as the central act of Sunday worship. They dreamt of the Church of England as a great network of eucharistic communities.

As Evangelicals and Anglo-Catholics have grown closer within the Church of England, so these two visions have married; and the offspring of their union has been a creature commonly known as the 'committed Christian'. The committed Christian is a regular communicant, attending a service on Sundays usually called Family Communion or, in churches with a Catholic tradition, Family Eucharist. The committed Christian participates in house groups, especially during Lent, but often at other times of the year as well. The committed Christian is willing to take a turn on the PCC, and also belongs to a sub-committee, perhaps dealing with fund-raising, children's work, or fabric repairs. The committed Christian is also on at least one rota – the cleaning rota, the brass rota, the rota for making coffee after the Family Communion, the flower rota, or the Sunday Sschool rota. The committed Christian belongs to some kind of fellowship that meets on one evening a month to hear a speaker, and has a summer outing. The committed Christian is willing to participate in occasional Saturday meetings, usually held at a Christian centre away from the parish, to discuss some aspect of parochial strategy. And the committed Christian plays some part in extra-parochial activities, such as the deanery synod or ecumenical gatherings of various kinds. At home, usually on the kitchen wall, the committed Christian pins up the page of the parish magazine that lists the calendar of events for the month; and it is a rare date when nothing is scheduled.

The modern cult of the committed Christian, although it has theological foundations, undoubtedly gains strength from the financial pressures on parishes. A church filled with committed Christians probably has little difficulty in raising the quota: the collection plate on Sunday is reasonably heavy, and fund-raising events run smoothly and profitably. So not unnaturally the numerous churches struggling to pay the quota admire, and even envy, them – and yearn to acquire some more committed Christians in their own ranks.

Thus for spiritual and material reasons alike the Church of England has come to equate success with bustle: the flourishing Christian community is a busy community.

It is well- known – indeed, it is blindingly obvious – that people, if they wish to be religious, are likely to choose a religion that accords with their social and cultural background. In my case the process was quite deliberate: I chose Christianity not because I regarded it as superior to other religions, but because I belong to a culture whose religious history is Christian; and I chose the Church of England because I am English. By the same logic it must also be true that people select a religious organization according to their temperament. For a few brief years in my twenties I quite enjoyed the bustle of modern parish life; or at least I did not especially resent having some kind of church meeting on most mid-week evenings. When I reached my mid- thirties I had wearied of it; and now in my early fifties I should have great difficulty belonging to a standard Anglican parish. By nature I am especially solitary and reclusive, preferring to spend most of my working and my leisure hours alone. But people with normal temperaments, and with normal jobs that bring them into constant contact with others, also want to spend the bulk of their evenings and weekends alone with their families. Thus modern Anglican bustle appeals only to quite a narrow portion of the population, while most people simply could not cope with being 'committed Christians'.

The ubiquity of the Family Communion both exemplifies the busy-ness of modern Anglicanism, and further narrows its appeal. Christ Church in Lancaster was an early exponent of this form of worship, eagerly adopting the new liturgy (Series 3, as it was then called) that provides an ideal framework. And when we started attending, we were overwhelmed by the sheer amount of activity: different people popping up to read lessons and say prayers; processions backwards and forwards along the aisle, first with the Bible, then with the bread and the wine, and finally with the collection; the choir, and sometimes a band, jumping up to sing bits of the service; boys and girls moving round the altar performing various esoteric functions; and the congregation itself being required to change its posture between sitting, kneeling and standing with irritating frequency. Two or three times in the course of all this the priest announced a time of silence but the atmosphere was too tense for any kind of reflection – which the priest himself must have sensed, because he generally cut the silences short.

My only previous experience of Anglican Sunday worship had been Matins in the 1950s at my grandmother's church in Dorchester, where the pace was slow and leisurely. But there was a further difference, which was more profound. At the end of Matins at Holy Trinity, Dorchester, everyone poured out into the sunshine or rain; and while most people went home, once a month a few slipped back into the church for a short 'said Communion'. The exclusivity of the Communion has been a feature of Christian worship since the earliest centuries; in the Ethiopian Orthodox Church only the very old and the very young receive the sacrament, because they alone are deemed 'pure'. The proponents of the Family Communion intended to break this down, and to some degree this has occurred. But the main consequence has been to discourage those who might appreciate some kind of Christian worship, but do not feel sufficiently pious or strong in faith to become communicants.

Indeed, I am inclined to think the damage goes much further than this. About ten years' ago I found myself entertaining Enoch Powell to lunch on behalf of a charity of which I am a trustee. After a discussion about Northern Island – in which he put forward a theory that the Protestants and Catholics are racially different, coming from different sides of the Sperrin Mountains – I steered the conversation onto religion. He described how in his early adulthood he was strongly atheist. His conversion to Christianity began when, out of a combination of boredom and discontent, he started attending Evensong. As he put it, Evensong 'allowed me to dip my toe in the water'. Perhaps in theory people should also be able to dip their toes into Communion; but in practice they do not and cannot. Many churches, aware of this problem, have introduced monthly 'family services', which often attract quite large numbers. Yet clergy frequently remark how few people graduate from family services to Family Communion – the spiritual gap is too large.

Andrew Brown, the self-declared atheist who writes an excellent column on the press in the *Church Times*, describes the Church of England as a 'club for nice people'. Anglican congregations are probably nicer today than ever before in history; and newcomers can be almost guaranteed a warm welcome. But while that niceness is utterly sincere and genuine, membership of the club carries a very high fee. Adding up the notes and coins they put in the collection plate, the money they spend at fund-raising events, and the contributions they make in kind to those events, few members can see much change from £500 a year, and many put in considerably more. Probably most Anglicans spend between five and ten hours a week on activities related to the church, including worship. And over and above all that, they are under pressure to remain consistently nice; Anglicans rarely, if ever, tell one another to 'fuck off' – at least within the confines of the club. A few people – a diminishing few – are willing to pay this fee; and some gain great satisfaction in doing so. But as the fee has gone up and up, so more and more people are staying out of the club.

Dear Rowan...

Chapter 4

✠

SOFTENING THE EDGES

Really good news

When I was a student at Durham University in 1969/70 – I lasted only a year before continuing my vocation as a hippie – I was persuaded by a Christian friend to attend a series of addresses given by the famous evangelist David Watson. Having already spent a year (a 'gap year', as it is now called) in India, where I became immersed in Hinduism and Jainism, I was regarded by my Christian friend as a spiritual seeker who was ripe for conversion to Christianity. My recollection is that David Watson's addresses were billed as the 'Good News Mission'; and certainly David Watson frequently assured us that his purpose was to impart good news.

The problem for me was that his news was bad. He informed us that we were all sinners, and deserved eternal punishment – and God would ensure that all non-Christians like me got their just deserts. That was nasty enough; but his solution to my young mind was even worse. He explained that Jesus Christ, who was 'literally' the son of God, died on the cross in order to take onto himself the punishment for our sins; and, if we put our faith in Jesus, we shall gain the benefit of this sacrifice. Once we have made this act of faith, we shall then be guided by the Holy Spirit, who is also divine, to obey God's commandments. Thus David Watson was asking me to betray my own intellect by accepting a set of utterly preposterous propositions, and then to become a moral automaton.

The grotesqueness of David Watson's message did,

however, stimulate me to study Christianity a little further. I wondered if all Christians shared his theology – if the most intelligent minds in Europe had for almost two millennia been duped by such nonsense. I soon found David Watson was an adherent of something called 'the substitutionary doctrine of the atonement', which many faithful Christians (including you, I think) also cannot stomach. Nonetheless, even the most rational and credible versions of Christianity appeared to rest on two implausible ideas. The first is that Jesus Christ was a historical figure who lived, died and rose again more or less as the Bible relates. While this is possible, the evidence seemed to me quite flimsy; it was certainly not strong enough to become the grounds for changing my entire way of life. The second, even more crucial idea is that there is a personal God whose actions can be influenced by the prayers people utter, by the rituals they perform, and by their moral behaviour. This, I concluded, amounted to little more than magic.

My main academic subject at Durham was anthropology; and at the time of grappling with David Watson's bad news I was also reading the works of Bronislaw Malinowski, one of the pioneers of anthropology who spent a couple of years on a Melanesian island studying the native way life. He made a sharp distinction between magic and religion. Magic, in his view, consists of human attempts to influence supernatural forces; and religion consists of human attempts to change and transform themselves, sometimes, but not invariably, in conformity to their understanding of the supernatural realm. This conception of religion had occurred to me in India during a month I spent with a group of Jain monks, wandering from village to village. The Jains are atheist, denying the existence of supernatural beings and forces,; and yet the monks were more devout – more religious – than any Christians I had ever met. Their aim is to attain complete inner, spiritual serenity, which expresses itself in perfect, selfless love for all living beings. Thus Jainism is – in Malinowski's definition – a religion that is completely free of all magical elements.

I became a Christian just over a year after David Watson's mission. I returned to India – accompanied by my future wife, whom I had met at Durham – after dropping out of my anthropology degree. My Christianity was, and still is, very Jain isn its intellectual and spiritual form; and a small community belonging to the ancient Orthodox church of India, which claims to have been founded by the apostle Thomas, was the agent of my conversion. Recognizing my intellectual stumbling-blocks, the priest leading this community suggested that I regard 'God' as signifying human perfection; he also said that, even if the Gospels are works of fiction, the figure of Jesus portrayed in them is an exemplar of perfect humanity. The key to the message of Jesus, according to the priest, is repentance, in the true sense of changing direction. Jesus, he said, invites us to stop pursuing happiness purely in terms of outward possessions and achievement, and to turn inwards, seeking happiness through spiritual means. The good news – the really good news – is that repentance actually works: over time repentant people become happy people.

The community leader himself actually held quite orthodox beliefs about the supernatural; and he claimed to have reached these beliefs not through being taught them by others, but through his own inner journey. At times through the past three decades I too have had inner experiences that seemed to point towards orthodoxy. Yet I have never been entirely convinced of this; and intellectual honesty compels me to remain agnostic – I simply do not know whether the supernatural beliefs of any religion are true or false. My central conviction, however, is stronger than ever: that religion offers the best, and ultimately the only, path to happiness. And that is the good news that I try to convey to people in my little parish of Upton. I am not myself blessed with a happy nature; but insofar as I enjoy any degree of happiness, I owe it to religion. And the nature of human happiness, as the Jains first showed me, is to want to share it with others. I do not mind what doctrines or beliefs about the supernatural that my parishioners hold; it is what they are, and what they are becoming, that matters to me.

In the eyes of many church-people my religion is not merely heretical, but non-existent. To them religion consists of beliefs about the supernatural, and Christianity is the particular set of supernatural beliefs summarized in the Nicene Creed – or whatever doctrinal formulae they happen to favour. And some would say that my doctrinal liberalism makes me unfit to serve as a priest in the Church of England. I have three responses. First, Christianity, in common with other religions, has a long mystical tradition; and the starting point for mystics is a humble recognition of one's lack of spiritual knowledge, combined with a deep yearning for spiritual transformation. Meister Eckhart, one of the greatest of Christian mystics, was found guilty of heresy precisely because, like the Orthodox priest who enabled me to become Christian, he reinterpreted the Gospel in interior terms, and denied the magical elements of Christian teaching.

My second response is that the stumbling blocks preventing me from accepting Christian orthodoxy are stumbling blocks for countless others also. It is not just eggheads and bookworms like that are liable to trip up on the concepts of the trinity, the incarnation and the redemption. The conversations recorded by David Hay and Kate Hunt in their Adult Spirituality Project show people of all educational backgrounds finding it impossible to square their own spiritual experiences with orthodoxy. Does the Church of England really want to exclude from its pews these honest spiritual explorers? The historic genius of the Church of England lay in its inclusiveness, embracing all who are sincere in their quest for truth and goodness. Perhaps people of my kind are like the Canaanite woman, only worthy of picking up crumbs from the table,; but it cannot be right to drive us away from the table itself. On the contrary, as the number capable of swallowing the full orthodox meal diminishes, so the crumb-eaters should be more warmly welcomed.

Thirdly, crumb-eaters may eventually become hungry for the full meal. I personally am quite content to remain on the floor amongst the crumbs, and expect to remain there until I die. And I am happy that so many of my parishioners are on the floor with me. Others, however, have spiritual experiences that enable them to understand and accept the Nicene Creed; and I do nothing to discourage them. Indeed, despite continuing to reject the kind of doctrinal Christianity preached by David Watson – and, in a somewhat different form, by you – I have over the years been the vehicle for quite a number of people coming to accept it.

Enjoyable religion

I became the priest at Upton in 1982, a few months after being ordained. The previous priest lived in the neighbouring village of Alconbury. At around the time of my ordination he announced to the bishop that he was no longer willing to minister in Upton because pastoral relations had broken down. I had lived in the area for about five years, and some people in Upton already knew me, and they asked the bishop if he would appoint me as their priest-in-charge. The bishop made clear to me that I would be unpaid – or 'non-stipendiary', in the constipated jargon of the Church. I was very happy with this. I had a full-time lectureship in Economics at Anglia Polytechnic in Cambridge, and was supervising at one of the University colleges,; and I enjoyed my work. Besides, I had always been determined not to become a burden on the laity by going on the Church's payroll. At the same time I liked the idea of having pastoral independence, rather than being a perpetual assistant curate, which is the fate of most unpaid priests.

The typical congregation in Upton was three or four – which in a village of about 150 people conformed to the national average of Anglican worshippers. One of the churchwardens and most of the PCC only attended church at festivals. And the church building itself was in an advanced state of disrepair, with the plaster dropping of the interior walls in lumps, and the tiles sliding off the roof. The Alconbury priest had made clear to the non-attending churchwarden and PCC members that they should be debarred from office. This was legally correct; but they regarded his attitude as high-handed and hostile. Here was clearly an ideal opportunity to try out my ultra-liberal approach to ministry.

Despite the negative advice I had received about general visiting during my training, I decided to visit every home in the parish; and I devoted Saturdays to the task. About half of the village consists of large houses, mostly quite new, and a few old. There are eight council houses built just after the War and the rest is a mobile home estate on the grounds of the old rectory. The social mix roughly reflects that of Britain as a whole – which is unusual, since most villages today are ghettos of the wealthy. It took me about six months to get round the whole village. At some point in most of the conversations my hosts would say something to the effect of: 'I can be a Christian without coming to church.' Behind the remark lay a combination of mild guilt and defiance; and it was uttered to forestall any attempt on my part to pressurize them into attending services. My reply invariably was: 'I agree' – which took them aback. And I sometimes mentioned my late father, who as a boy at Eton, where every morning they sing the *Magnificat* with its strictures against the rich and powerful, had rejected the Church as organized hypocrisy, yet in his generosity and kindness he was an exemplary Christian. And I usually concluded by saying: 'Only come to church services if you enjoy them and get some benefit from them.'

But this last remark begged two obvious and awkward questions, which fortunately no one asked, and for which I had not devised any satisfactory answers. First, how can a church service possibly be enjoyable? And secondly, what benefit can anyone possibly get from it? In search of inspiration I went into the Anglia Polytechnic library, and revised my anthropology. Emile Durkheim, whose writings had excited me even more than those of Malinowski, said that the purpose of religious rituals is to transmit social values; and if those values are 'functional', fostering social harmony, then people will enjoy the rituals. So by implication a church service in Upton will be both pleasant and beneficial if people feel drawn closer to one another. As a working hypothesis I felt happy about this, with one proviso: that Upton services should transmit spiritual values, rather than social ones. Spiritual values should, of course, include social ones, since the person directed towards inner change in the image of Christ is directed towards harmony with others, but the term 'spiritual' indicates the process by which religion operates.

The main fruit of enjoyable and beneficial religion should be in the lives of the people attending it. This is a pretty stringent test: as priest of Upton, I should only count myself successful if the members of my congregation, year by year, become happier and better. But Durkheim's writings suggest an even more stringent test. He believed that 'functional' religion, even if only a minority participates in it, will make the whole community function better. Thus, good worship in Upton church should benefit the entire village; in the metaphors of Jesus, it should act as salt in food, or yeast in bread. Yikes! As I sat in Anglia Poly library, I wondered about sending my resignation to the bishop, on the grounds that the challenge of parochial ministry was beyond me.

Twenty years on Upton has become – as newcomers consistently testify – an exceptionally friendly village, with comparatively few of the kind of squabbles and rivalries that tend to mar small communities. Those coming regularly to services at the parish church, comprising around 12 per cent of the population, seem in general to enjoy themselves, as do the occasional churchgoers, comprising around 50 per cent. But it is impossible to measure the church's contribution to the village's well-being. And while I am aware that some members of the congregation are happier and more content than when I first knew them, neither they nor I can unravel the church's effect on their lives from all the other influences. So the Durkheimian tests of successful ministry are like chaos theory: while it is possible that a butterfly flapping its wings in one part of the world may eventually trigger a typhoon in another part, the links between cause and effect are beyond our powers of perception.

Our staple pattern of worship consists of Evensong once a fortnight, using the original form produced by Cranmer in 1549; this is what the present generation of middle-aged and elderly people in Upton seems to want. Cranmer's Evensong is very similar to the later 1662 version, except that it has no general confession at the beginning. While I do not deny the possibility of people turning back and facing the wrong way again, I am highly dubious about the value of self-abasing words of contrition at the outset of regular worship. I personally would like to participate in Cranmer's Evensong until I die, and if there is a heaven, I look forward to an eternity of summer evenings in an English village church, with the sound of the versicles and responses in my immortal ears. But I fear that over the next twenty or thirty years the taste for Cranmer will steadily diminish. Most members of the present congregation became familiar with Cranmer's cadences in childhood, as I did in the company of my grandmother in Holy Trinity, Dorchester but Cranmer had largely been abandoned by the early 1970s. Besides, as adult churchgoing has diminished, and as Sunday schools have shrunk or closed, fewer and fewer children have had any experience of Anglican worship. So Cranmer means nothing to people under about forty-five; and updated versions of Cranmer, such as the services in the Alternative Service Book, also lack resonance.

In addition to Evensong we have six festival services in the course of the year: Christmas, Mothering Sunday, Easter, a mid-summer festival celebrating gardens and flowers, Harvest, and Remembrance. A similar annual round of festivals can be found not only in other branches of Christianity, but also in the other religions of the world. It seems that human beings have a deep, inherent urge to mark the year with religious festivals, and to use these festivals to express perennial feelings about the family, children, parenthood, death and the dead, food, and nature. So their attraction does not depend on childhood resonance – although this can help. My impression is that these festivals are growing in popularity throughout the country, or at least not diminishing. The trick is to enable those coming, especially those who do not come to regular Sunday services, to feel comfortable and this means never criticizing them for their infrequency of attendance, never urging them to make a bigger commitment, being unashamedly populist with the music, not requiring them to say the Creed or anything with significant doctrinal content, and giving clear directions about when to stand and sit. The services should not be slick performances that have clearly required lengthy rehearsal; on the contrary, they are better if they are quite homely and even a little ramshackle. The only way to transmit spiritual and social values is to engender feelings of spiritual contentment and social ease.

My hunch is that, if I survive into old age, I shall witness communal worship at Upton becoming confined to the festivals. I also anticipate that more people will wander into the church for quiet contemplation. And while some larger churches in suburbs and towns will retain a full programme of weekly worship, festivals and individual visits will in the next generation form the bulk of church attendance. Indeed, this seems quite a natural pattern of religion. In India, for example, almost everyone is caught up in the great annual festivals such as Holi and Diwali, and people visit their local temple from time to time as they feel moved. Similarly in pre-Reformation Europe, while the Mass was said weekly or even daily in most churches, the laity was actually excluded by means of the rood screen; and lay participation only occurred at Christmas, Easter, Rogation, Corpus Christi, and so on. At the same time people frequently popped into their parish church to say a prayer and travellers poked their heads into every church they passed to offer a prayer to St Christopher, whose picture was usually on the wall opposite the door. In this regard the Ethiopian Orthodox Church remains gloriously unreformed to this day.

When it comes to the 'rites of passage' – as the anthropologist van Gennep called the rituals marking the human life-cycle – the Church of England is at a crossroads. Confirmation at puberty is rapidly disappearing: as recently as 1960 almost 200,000 people were confirmed, whereas now there is barely a sixth of that number. Baptism of babies is also becoming much less common: in 1960 over a half of the babies born in England were baptized in the Church of England, but now the figure is falling towards one tenth. In modern Britain the private rituals and markers relating to childhood and growing up – such as birthday parties, present-giving at Christmas, going clubbing for the first time, passing the driving test, and so on – have become much more extensive than in the past; and schools provide many public rituals. So in effect the Church has been squeezed out; and nothing can, or should, be done. Weddings and funerals, however, represent a genuine challenge, which the Church of England may either win or lose, depending on how it responds.

The decline in the proportion of people getting married

seems to be over, and marriage may even be gaining in popularity. But the proportion of marriages taking place in the Church of England has halved in the past forty years, and is now barely a third. The change in the law, which allows attractive places like stately homes and smart hotels to be used for weddings, has stiffened the competition. The Church of England's own laws, allowing only residents of the parish to be married in a particular church, do not help. Nor does the awkwardness of some clergy towards couples who do not regularly attend church. And the marriage service itself has a lot of doctrinal content that many couples cannot honestly stomach. Most funerals still have a clergyman officiating. But this is not, as in the past, because the priest has been giving pastoral support to the family involved, and is therefore the person to whom the family immediately turns. Families generally turn first to a funeral director; and funeral directors find it convenient to call on the clergy to officiate. Funeral directors also find it more convenient to organize the entire funeral service at a crematorium, rather than have the service at a church. Thus the religious content of most modern funerals is pretty thin.

If the Church of England wishes to be true to its inclusive roots, it must fight back with gusto and imagination. Obviously the Church's laws on weddings should be greatly relaxed and there seem to be some tentative moves already in this direction. And people should have far greater choice over the contents of the services, so the contents can be matched to their own spiritual understanding and needs. The core of the wedding service consists of the vows and the exchanging of rings; and the core of the funeral service is the committal of the body. Beyond that everything should be open to discussion. In Upton we recently had the funeral of an atheist lady, who stipulated in her will that she wanted an atheist funeral – in church. Her sons, with a little guidance from me, put together a wonderful service, with readings from Shakespeare, Wordsworth and A A Milne, favourite music played on CD, and little eulogies given by members of her family. A few weeks later we had the wedding of a Buddhist and lapsed Roman Catholic, with oriental music and readings from the *Dhammapada*. The strangest feature of both these services was how very Anglican they still seemed; their physical context somehow seemed to imprint both the planning of the services and their enactment with an indelible Anglican stamp.

At present the resources available for devising more imaginative weddings and funerals, and also for imaginative celebrations of the festivals, are scant. The simple reason is that there is scant demand for them, so publishers, record companies and the like have no incentive to produce them. And many clergy would, of course, regard my suggestions – and my practice – as sacrilege. But compare services in churches today with those of a hundred, two hundred, three hundred, four hundred and five hundred years ago. The changes in each century have been huge; and every change has had numerous opponents crying, 'Sacrilege!' The stimulus for change has been people's changing need and demands. The Church of England has declined when it has refused to meet people's needs, and it has flourished when it has responded; its genius has lain in its capacity to respond while remaining true to itself. My long years of involvement with publishing assure me that, if and when the Church of England starts to respond to present needs, the resources will quickly become available.

Matrix ministry

When I finally felt ready to undertake a degree, I decided to study Economics, with a particular emphasis on business. And I chose Lancaster University, partly because it had a good department in this field, and partly because it had an excellent Religious Studies department, under the prophetic leadership of Ninian Smart. My main interest was, of course, religion; and I wanted to be able to read the books in the Religious Studies section of the library, and attend some of the lectures given by Professor Smart and his colleagues. But this would be my recreation and pleasure and besides, I never wanted to earn my living from religion, as I feared this would spoil my enjoyment of it. The attraction of Economics was that, while religion is concerned with the inner lives of human beings, economics issues form the key to their outer lives – and I wanted to try and understand the connections between the two.

In my first year at Lancaster I took a course in business organization. The central part of this course was concerned with 'organizational trees', which looked like family trees, but in fact were concerned with decision-making. Each level on the tree was a position or rank in the business hierarchy; and decisions were reached and implemented by means of information flowing upwards, and authority flowing downwards. This is also, of course, how an army operates; and the lecturer declared that, just as an army should be efficient at fighting on the battle field, a business should be efficient at fighting in the market place.

The university is on a campus to the south of the city and my wife and I bought a little terraced house near an old cotton mill in the heart of the city. During that year I borrowed books from the Religious Studies section on the Church of England, and took them home to read in the evenings, in order to prepare myself for confirmation – and to make sure I really wanted to be confirmed. I soon learnt, both from reading and from discussion with our parish priest, that the Church of England has its own organizational tree; and like businesses and the army, information is supposed to flow upwards, with decisions flowing downwards. Indeed, the comparison with the army is quite precise. An archbishop is like a general, with a province the equivalent of an entire army; a bishop is a brigadier, whose brigade is his diocese; an archdeacon is a colonel, with an archdeaconry as a regiment; a rural dean is a major, a parish priest a captain, and an assistant curate a lieutenant. The laity form the other ranks: churchwardens are non-commissioned officers; PCC members are corporals; and privates form the congregations, lining up for parade every Sunday morning. By this analogy, you as Archbishop of Canterbury are commander-in-chief.

Since I completed my degree in 1976 the world of business has changed almost out of recognition. Most of the ranks in business hierarchies have been abolished, in a process known by the ugly term 'delayerization'. And more and more decisions have been devolved to those who implement them, in a process known as 'empowerment'. This, of course, has reduced costs and computers have greatly aided the flow of information within business organizations, making many of the middle layers of management redundant. But the main reason is that people function more efficiently, and they are more highly motivated, if they have a high degree of freedom and personal responsibility. Various new organizational charts have been devised to achieve empowerment; and amongst creative businesses, such as film companies, advertising agencies, software designers, and the like, the most popular has been the 'matrix model' – a matrix having horizontal lines, with vertical lines cutting through them. The horizontal lines are teams of people with complementary abilities and skills, who are given projects; and they carry the projects through from start to finish. The vertical lines are those in overall charge and their main tasks are to form the teams and assign them their projects, to ensure that the members of the teams are fit for their tasks, providing training as required, and to monitor the progress of each project.

As an economist I have watched these changes both with professional interest, and with instinctive approval, because I am the kind of free spirit that thrives within a matrix organization. As a churchwarden and then as a priest, I have had a further reason for fascination. While the present Church of England is an army-style hierarchy, I have learnt that its historic structure consists of two inter-connected matrices – one within the parish, and the other within the diocese. Thus the Church of England understood matrix management a millennium before business theorists did. And, of course, vestiges of this historic structure remain.

At the head of the English parochial organization, possibly since its inception in Saxon times, was a team consisting of the priest and the churchwardens; and together they carried ultimate responsibility for the parish. The genius of the system lay in three factors. First, they were locally appointed: while the people elected the churchwardens, the priest was chosen by a patron, normally the lord of the manor, and the lord of the manor, whose own position was much easier if the serfs respected him, was likely to be sensitive to their wishes and needs. Thus the priest and churchwardens had independent authority, which meant they tended to operate as a team, rather than the priest bossing the churchwardens. Also their local accountability meant they had strong incentive to succeed in their roles. Secondly, their respective tasks were enormous, so they could only succeed by drawing on the abilities and energy of others in the parish. The churchwardens, in addition to various secular responsibilities, broadly had charge of the church building; and the frequent embellishing and extending of English churches bear witness to the way in which churchwardens drew on the manual labour of the poorer parishioners, and the wealth of the richer ones. The enormous complexity and artistry of medieval festivals demonstrate that the priests were equally good at drawing on parishioners' creative flair. In terms of the matrix metaphor the priest and the churchwardens formed a horizontal line at the head of the parish organization, and thence formed two vertical lines; teams of parishioners convened by them then formed a series of horizontal lines.

Within the English diocese each parish formed a horizontal line, enjoying a high degree of autonomy. In addition to choosing its own churchwardens and priest, it had charge of its own finances, land and buildings. Also it could to a remarkable degree choose its own style of worship: in medieval times there were several different missals circulating in England, and ways of celebrating festivals and rites of passage varied considerably from parish to parish. There was a single vertical line in a diocese with the bishop at its head. Aidan, the first bishop of

Northumbria, was the model for English episcopacy that, despite many abuses, remained essentially intact until modern times. He toured his diocese regularly, preaching the Christian faith, and forming new congregations. He then encouraged suitable local men to offer themselves as priests, and he trained them at his monastery in Lindisfarne. Similarly the role of the Victorian bishop was still mainly confined to selecting people for ordination, supervising their training, and monitoring their progress.

It is perhaps hardly surprising that in that in the twentieth century the matrix style of working gave way to one-dimensional hierarchy. In industry the small workshop and factory yielded to the vast corporation, and in politics the government created huge bureaucracies to run education and health care. The leaders of these new organisations, business directors and politicians alike, believed that clear chains of command led to efficiency, so the Church of England, in trying to keep up with the time, decided to operate in the same way. This was made easier by the various ranks that the Church already possessed, from archbishop downwards, so people at all levels of the Church could quite easily slip into a hierarchical way of thinking. And it made considerable amendments to its laws in order to enact and legitimise this change.

In the past twenty years, since businesses have been replacing hierarchy with various forms of empowerment, the British economy has been transformed from stagnation to dynamism. While business and religion deal with quite distinct spheres of human life, the same organizational principles apply to both; and so it is a matter of utmost urgency that the Church of England rediscovers its historic capacity for empowering people. Much as I feel nostalgic for the distant past, we cannot precisely restore the old ways, because circumstances have changed so hugely; rather, we must find new ways of applying old wisdom. And it seems to me there are four aspects to this challenge.

The first concerns the way in which priests are appointed to parishes. Few patrons now are local, and many take little interest in their role. As a result bishops now appoint most clergy to parishes, merely seeking the patron's approval. This episcopal power has been greatly extended by the way in which bishops have stretched the intentions of the Pastoral Measure of 1983. The part entitled 'Miscellaneous, Administrative and General' allows bishops to suspend the patron's powers, and to appoint a 'priest-in-charge' on a limited-term contract. It was envisaged that this would only be used as a temporary arrangement, while some new pastoral scheme was being hatched, but across large swathes of the countryside it has become virtually permanent. All this should be changed, so that the power of appointment of clergy is returned to parishes. There is a danger, which has often been pointed out to me, that parish priests would become the servants of the small clique of church members that appointed them; hence they would be even more inward-looking, and give even less time to those who only occasionally or never attend services. I am unconvinced of this, since most church members are eager for their congregation to expand, and so would welcome an outward-looking priest. Besides, it would be good to include the church's occasional attenders in choosing a priest.

The second concerns the functions of the clergy. Appendix 2 of Schedule 3 of the Synodical Government Measure of 1969, contains in small print these words: 'the minister of the parish shall be chairman of the parochial church council.' Thus the minister, and not the churchwardens, is made the apex of parochial administration; and the consequences are huge and devastating. The horizontal line at the top of the parish matrix is turned into a vertical line, with the priest as the boss and the churchwardens as assistants and this is in turn engenders a hierarchical mentality throughout the parish. Moreover, the priest's spiritual ministry is overlain by administrative demands – and the rural priest, with several PCCs to chair, is utterly overwhelmed. Of course, some priests today are excellent administrators, because the Church's selection process now favours such people,; but it is rare for good administrators also to be good pastors. The role of the priest, as priest, is to organize and conduct worship, and to offer spiritual care to the people – and anything detracting from this should be abandoned.

The third concerns the nature of the relationship of priests with rural parishes. The priests of thriving churches in suburbs and market towns are clearly worth every penny of their stipends, especially if they are free from administrative tasks. And priests in poor urban parishes, where few attend worship, can also do a huge amount of good, both helping individuals, and providing encouragement to the community as a whole. But rural priests covering several parishes are an absurdity: on Sundays they rush from one service to another, with barely time to smile at parishioners, and while they may give pastoral support to individuals, they cannot become pastors to their parishes, for the simple reason that, with the exception of the parish where the vicarage happens to be located, they do not live in their parishes. It is a common experience that a rural parish functions most successfully during a long interregnum, when local people can organize themselves freely. They quickly start using their various abilities to far greater effect, and find great satisfaction in doing so. In some cases one of the churchwardens, who happens to have spiritual insight, becomes the *de facto* pastor, convening informal teams to organize worship and to ensure people are visited; in other cases one or two well-respected people, who have no formal title, take this role. Clergy are then invited for particular purposes, such as conducting Communion, officiating at weddings and funerals, and presiding at major festivals. There would, of course, be nothing new in this: frequently in past centuries rural parishes have not had resident priests, often because they were too poor to support them, and there were itinerant priests whom parishes paid as they needed them. I myself am a modern example, since, although I draw no money from Upton, I currently earn about £1,200 per year from preaching and officiating elsewhere, augmenting my income from writing, teaching and financial management. There are more and more people like me with 'portfolios' of jobs; and freelance priestly activity makes a happy addition to a portfolio.

The fourth concerns the relationship of the parish church to the parishioners. The men in medieval times labouring to erect steeples, construct aisles, and extend chancels were not for the most part communicants, and the families donating gold and silver, with which stone was purchased and skilled craftsmen were hired to fashion tracery and gargoyles, were mostly ignorant of the Nicene Creed. Similarly the groups who sang carols round the village at Christmas, and who cooked food and brewed ale for the harvest supper in the nave, were drawn from any and every cottage, house and hovel. Yet all these people were religious, and were acknowledged by the Church as religious. While the hierarchical style of ministry tends to be exclusive, deterring any that cannot conform to its particular demands, the matrix style of ministry is by its nature inclusive, drawing in everyone who is willing to be drawn in. Indeed, the greatest virtue of matrix ministry is its evangelism – the kind of open-hearted and open-minded evangelism to which most people can respond.

The Upton way

As it became clear that the bishops were stretching the Pastoral Measure of 1983 to accumulate more power for themselves over clergy deployment, some commentators reacted with indignation. The *Spectator* published an especially fierce article, accusing the bishops of both duplicity and megalomania. The bishops I have met recently – only a handful, since I am rarely invited to events where bishops are present – have not struck me as putative Hitlers, or even as economists with the truth. They sincerely believe in ecclesiastical hierarchy and in my view it is morally quite proper for them to use the law in accordance with their principles. I believe with equal conviction in the traditional 'matrix' principles of church organization and, when I have given talks on the matter, I have found that most lay people and many clergy are inclined to agree with me. And at Upton we too have tried to stretch the law – in accordance with our principles.

In the mid 1980s, as the quota started to rise steeply, the Upton PCC asked to see the diocesan treasurer; and one evening the treasurer sent his deputy, who had to drive thirty miles through dark Fen lanes. The PCC members explained that they were spending so much on restoring the fabric of the church that they could not afford to meet the quota. The deputy treasurer responded with a well-practised homily on their moral obligation to support the parochial ministry; and he concluded that 'the church is the people, not the buildings.' Like most senior clergy and lay officers using this well-worn phrase, he meant by 'people' the clergy. But the PCC members missed this subtlety, and replied that 'without the building there would be no people.' They also pointed out that, since I received no stipend and had full-time secular work, they were responsible for running the parish – so their extra contribution to parochial ministry was in time rather than in money. Then a farm labourer asked bluntly: 'What happens if we don't pay the quota?' The deputy treasurer blustered, and the labourer repeated the question. Finally the deputy treasurer said: 'Nothing. There is no legal obligation to pay the quota.' At the next PCC meeting, the members decided to stop paying the quota and Upton has not paid it since.

The PCC was no doubt influenced by my own views on the folly of the quota system, which I had already made public in newspaper articles. But in these articles I also strongly advocated the creation of a fund to subsidize ministry in poor urban areas; and I said to the PCC members that I would only support their decision if they agreed to set aside a significant amount each year for charity – which could be diverted to such a fund, if it were ever established. They correctly observed that Upton was not a rich village, since most of the people living in mobile homes, who constitute half the population, were surviving on the state pension. Nonetheless, they accepted my condition.

In 1990 the Bishop of Ely convened an informal group to help him formulate a policy on the twin issues of finance and clergy deployment. To his credit he said that he wanted to hear a variety of views, and he asked me to join the group. The other members were senior clerics in the diocese, including the cathedral dean, and senior lay people such as one of the General Synod representatives. Far from holding different opinions, they were all firmly committed to hierarchy – at least in these matters. Thus while the bishop should listen to local views on the numbers and allocation of clergy, the bishop alone should make the final decisions; the quota should then be set at whatever figure was necessary to fund the bishop's decisions. My views on parish autonomy were dismissed as 'congregationalist'; and the General Synod representative described my appeals to the traditions of the Church of England as 'obscurantist'.

It was a year later that the bishop refused to renew my licence as priest-in-charge of Upton and this led to the next stage in Upton's ecclesiastical odyssey.

Since that time Upton has had no official parish priest, and I function entirely at the churchwardens' invitation. The parish's legal protection lies in a combination of the Pastoral Measure of 1983, and a piece of legislation passed in 1986 quaintly entitled the Patronage (Benefices) Measure. Since bishops have made such extravagant use of their power under the Pastoral Measure to suspend the role of patrons, there is now no legal impediment to a parish remaining in permanent interregnum. If a parish wants this, it now has the ability, under the Patronage (Benefices) Measure, to veto any priest that the bishop may propose. The intention of the Measure was to put the bishop firmly at the centre of the process of appointing priests, and thence further clip the wings of patrons, but the procedures for consulting churchwardens unintentionally give them the right to stall the appointment process indefinitely. Technically speaking the Measure only refers to vicars and rectors who would have the 'freehold'; but as David Parrott and David Field, experts on church law, wrote in a recent Grove booklet entitled *Situation Vacant*, there is an obligation on bishops to follow the same procedure in regard to permanent priests-in-charge.

Upton is now in the midst of a further stage in its odyssey, which may be the most important. After a year of detailed discussion we have decided in effect to disband the PCC, and to replace it with a charitable trust whose trustees are elected by the whole village – regardless of whether they are baptized or are communicants. The churchwardens are *ex officio* trustees. There are two reasons for this change, one negative and the other positive. The negative reason is that any parish is potentially vulnerable to being abolished by a pastoral scheme and made part of a larger parish, and the procedures for this occurring give remarkably little voice to the churchwardens and parishioners. To my knowledge there is no immediate threat of this. But it is probable that financial pressures over the coming years will force rural dioceses to bring more and more parishes under each priest, until priests are utterly swamped by administrative tasks. It may then become tempting to reduce these tasks by merging parishes. By holding its financial assets in a separate trust, Upton could continue to operate *de facto* as an independent parish. I hope that, if and when rural dioceses consider such schemes, they will recognize the absurdity of destroying ancient parishes for the administrative convenience of the clergy, and instead press for the abolition of the law requiring the priest to be chairman of each PCC – but, given the Church of England's track record in recent decades, I feel anxious.

The positive and more important reason is evangelistic. Since most of the PCC members are not communicants, we want to make honest men and women of them, and since most of the residents of the village do not see themselves as members of the Church of England, and yet feel attached to Upton church, we want to enfranchise them. This constitutional change gives an important religious message: that the church is for all who want to grow in goodness and truth – to grow in Christ's image – and to join with others who have the same purpose. There may be a few in Upton, though I cannot name them, who exalt malice and falsehood, and there are some who are fairly indifferent to spiritual and moral values. But such people are highly unlikely to exercise their right to vote for trustees, let alone become trustees themselves. Most people have at least some spiritual and moral aspirations and they can now be fully integrated into the church.

There are two alternative legal mechanisms for achieving this change. The first is simply not to elect the PCC and, according both to common sense and to a reasonable interpretation of section 84 of the Pastoral Measure, its powers would revert to the churchwardens, from whom they were originally taken in 1921. The second is for the AGM to decide that the PCC should have only two members, who would automatically be the churchwardens. We have taken advice from one of the top church lawyers in the country. While both mechanisms are probably sound, he says that the second is safer. Thus the churchwardens now work with the other trustees in the exercise of their powers. Indeed, since the trust holds the financial assets, the churchwardens are as closely bound to the other trustees as they were to the PCC. Although its implications are more profound, the relationship between the churchwardens and the trust is legally quite similar to that between the chapter of a cathedral and the 'Friends' of the cathedral who raise most of the cash.

Over the past decade numerous people from parishes around England haveing written to me expressing their frustration at the current way in which the parochial system functions, and exploring the possibility of their parish following Upton's example. Most of these correspondents have been lay people, but a few have been clergy. In my reply I have been compelled to warn them of the opposition that they are likely to encounter from their diocesan authorities. And I have added that in the face of such opposition it is extremely difficult for parishioners to remain united. While they may all agree in principle, some will fall away when the first tough letter arrives from the archdeacon and few will have the stomach for arguments with the diocese's legal advisers – which has been a recurring feature of the Upton odyssey. Most of the correspondents have eventually decided to do nothing, usually because they themselves are reluctant to rebel. Some have discussed possible changes with fellow parishioners but, while they warm to them, most prefer a quiet life. Six parishes have actually gone some distance down the Upton way but only one is still moving. Those near the top of the ecclesiastical tree cling to their authority with great tenacity and their determination is doubtless strengthened by their sense of being officers in a great army with God as supreme commander. By this analogy, the parishioners of Upton are mutineers, and I am the treacherous lieutenant who incited them – and mutiny must be ruthlessly suppressed. It is small wonder that few are willing to join us.

But what if bishops allowed parishes to follow the Upton way, or to travel on whatever parts of it they wanted? What if they gave parishes the option of being a matrix rather than the bottom of a hierarchy? Perhaps parishioners are so comfortable and contented with their position that none would take the option. If so, then in my view the Church of England's decline will continue. My hunch is that there would be a trickle, then a stream, then a river, and finally a torrent of parishes turning themselves into matrices. Although many clergy would initially be anxious, they would soon find themselves relishing their own liberation – their liberation to fulfil their vocation more fully and more creatively. In the nineteenth century Cardinal Newman incurred the wrath of the Vatican, and there was even talk of his being a heretic, because he argued that ultimate authority in the Church lies with the people. In their hearts I suspect that most senior members of the Church of England side with Newman against the Vatican. The Upton way is simply the practical application of Newman's principle.

Chapter 5

✠

CANTERBURY PILGRIMS

When an Archbishop of Canterbury is enthroned, he is surrounded by the symbolism of hierarchy. Indeed, the new primate is presented not merely as a commander-in-chief, but as a monarch. But like the actual monarchy in Britain, this ecclesiastical monarchy is largely constitutional, with little executive and no legislative power. Of course, as the bishop of the diocese of Canterbury, you have all the power over clergy appointments that diocesan bishops have acquired during the past half century, but you have little time to exercise it, and assistant bishops do so on your behalf. As archbishop of the southern province of England, and as senior archbishop of the whole of England, there are few levers in your hands.

Unlike the monarch, however, the Archbishop of Canterbury has a great deal of influence – if he has the insight and charisma to exert it. You are generously blessed with both qualities. So I have little doubt that by the end of your tenure the Church of England will bear your imprint. I am also confident that you yourself will remain unimpressed by the regal trappings of your job, seeing yourself as the leader of a pilgrimage, rather than as a ruler.

There are already many strident voices telling you what direction to take. Some want you to march purposefully up the mountain of moral and doctrinal purity, where no practising homosexual can follow, and from which heretics are hurled into oblivion. Others want you to saunter into the lush valley of tolerance. As an ardent heretic who advocates homosexual weddings, my preference is for the valley. But in this letter I am counselling a kind of honest reticence on these matters. While there can be little harm in re-stating your personal views, which are already quite well known, it would achieve nothing to try and press your views on others. On the contrary, you would be expending energy and good will on disputes that cannot be won, because people's views are too entrenched – and which, even if they were won, would make little difference to ordinary people's lives.

There are other voices urging you to march at the head of the whole nation, asserting yourself as its moral guide. As someone who tends to share your political views – although I think I am more libertarian than you – I respect and relish your pronouncements on the issues of the day. And, while many church people tend to sound rather shrill or grumpy on political and social matters, your words invariably display a lively understanding of the modern world, as well as intellectual clarity. So you carry respect, and have a palpable impact on public opinion. But like anyone occupying a high office, you owe your authority to the institution that you lead. If that institution continues to crumble, even your wisest pronouncements will start to be met with wry scepticism. 'If he can't run the Church properly,' people will ask, 'what right has he to tell us how the country should be run?' The answer is that you will have no right.

My concern is not the direction in which you lead the

pilgrimage, but the way in which others are invited to join. Fewer and fewer people travel with the Church of England because we put such stringent conditions on who is allowed to travel with us, so more and more people reject our invitation, and go their own way. As it is within parishes that our invitation is offered, it is within parishes that we must alter the invitation's terms, so in this letter I have made practical, down-to-earth proposals on how this may be done. The essence of these proposals is to set people in the parishes free. Like leaders of all organizations, bishops and senior clergy tend to think that they must make things happen – they must take the initiatives. I am urging you and your colleagues to resist this urge, and instead to allow things to happen – you must take away the constraints.

The only other parts of the Anglican Communion familiar to me beyond England are the churches in Uganda and Sudan. In both countries parishes operate in much the same way that I am proposing for England; broadly speaking, they follow the old English way, rather than the present way and, they flourish. I must confess to being badly informed about the province of Wales, which you have led with such distinction, but my scant knowledge indicates that the trauma of disestablishment in the early twentieth century saved it from becoming unduly centralized and bureaucratic, and its parishes have retained a good deal of freedom – and as a result it has actually become more vigorous, at least compared with other denominations. So I like to think that you are already in sympathy with much of what I write.

The major constraints on the mission and ministry of England's parishes are legal and financial. While legal and financial changes could not in themselves bring about a transformation in the Church's fortunes, they are necessary conditions for transformation. In relation to the entire panoply of ecclesiastical law, the legal changes required are quite small but their effects would be huge. In particular I propose four changes, three of which are amendments to Schedule 3 of the Synodical Government Measure of 1969. First, the church electoral roll should be open to any adult resident of the parish, and anyone outside the parish who is a habitual worshipper at the church. Secondly, anyone on the electoral roll should also be eligible for election as churchwarden and to the PCC. Thirdly, the PCC should elect its chairman; and an ordained priest should not be eligible. The fourth change relates to the Patronage (Benefices) Measure whose wording should be amended to give churchwardens a more central role in the process of clergy appointments.

The financial changes are even simpler, and yet would also have a disproportionately large effect. It would be unnecessarily complicated, and also burdensome to parishioners, to return to the old system in which parishes paid their own priest directly. Instead, each parish, – or, in rural areas, each group – should have a quota whose main component should consist of the stipend, pension contribution and housing cost of the priest. There should be an additional component comprising the parish's share of diocesan costs – which include the diocese's payments to central funds – insofar as historic resources do not cover these. A parish or group of parishes could opt to pay both parts of the quota, and thence have a stipendiary priest, or it could join with an adjoining parish or group to share a priest, or it could opt to pay only the second component of the quota and not have a stipendiary priest. Some rural dioceses in some areas have already begun to move slowly in this direction; if the Church Commissioners were to give encouragement, it would happen much faster. In the process the perpetual financial crisis facing dioceses would be permanently solved. I should add that the central funds should include an annual sum for subsidizing poor parishes, especially in urban areas.

As the constitutional head of the Church of England, you cannot simply wave a sceptre, and demand such changes. But if you were to make clear that you wanted the 'culture' of the Church of England to shift, in order to liberate the spiritual gifts and creative abilities of parishioners, I am sure that these simple amendments to the law and to financial administration would prove quite easy to enact. After all, while the Church of England remains locked into a hierarchical culture, I cannot imagine any bishop or senior cleric actually declaring: 'The gifts and abilities of parishioners should remain closely controlled, and only exercised with express clerical permission.' Has not the Charismatic movement, for all its occasional fanaticism, reminded the Church that the Spirit blows where it wills?

While my heresy is so extreme that I prefer to call myself (in Leslie Weatherhead's august company) an agnostic rather than a theist, I am aware that a deliberate policy to invite other agnostics into parish life needs a degree of theological justification. Those opposed to liberals, especially liberals like me who regard other religions such as Hinduism and Buddhism as equal to Christianity, usually quote the words ascribed to Jesus in John's Gospel: 'No one comes to the Father but by me.' Bishop John Robinson, a great New Testament scholar, became an acquaintance of mine, and something of a mentor, in the final months of his life. He presented to me a copy of what he regarded as his finest book, *Truth is Two-Eyed* in which he argues that this saying should be interpreted in the light of John's opening verses, which provides the theological prism through which the rest of the Gospel should be interpreted. Jesus is identified with the eternal *Logos*, the divine Word that is the agent of all creation, and is present throughout creation. Thus we should expect to find that all people, of any religion or none, possess an innate knowledge of the divine; the path of Christ is to deepen that knowledge. To be honest, I do not wholly subscribe to this argument, partly because I am dubious about the notion of an eternal *Logos*, and partly because it is implicitly patronizing towards other religions. But, as an interpretation of John's Gospel, it seems an entirely correct and orthodox.

So, to sum up this entire letter in orthodox theological terms – let the Church of England once again learn to discern and embrace the divine Word in every man, woman and child in every parish.

AFTERWORD – ROWAN'S ENDORSEMENTS

I wrote this book in three weeks, immediately before and after Rowan Williams was declared the new Archbishop of Canterbury. The publisher then sent the manuscript to him, asking for any comments he may wish to make. In August Rowan Williams replied, saying that it is 'very good indeed ... all power to your elbow.' The letter also included some complimentary remarks about previous books I have written.

The publisher had also circulated it to a number of Bishops. In September Rowan wrote a second letter withdrawing the earlier endorsement. A Bishop had contacted Rowan to say that my book was liable 'to cause explosive reactions', and that Rowan's 'enthusiastic endorsement' would be 'embarrassing'. Rowan reassured the publisher that 'I still think it's a good book', and asked to alter his endorsement to: 'A bold and controversial agenda for the Church, which I shall want to ponder carefully.'

In October Rowan asked the publisher to withdraw the second endorsement.

I do not tell this tale to embarrass Rowan Williams. In fact, I think it puts him personally in a good light. His willingness to defer to the anxieties of others illustrates his approval and enjoyment of diversity of opinions. I did not infer that he necessarily agreed with the proposals contained in this book; rather, he wanted them to be heard and debated. His willingness to defer to the anxieties of the Bishop illustrates his sensitivity. His wish to withdraw all endorsement came in the wake of severe criticism of him from influential Evangelical figures in the Church of England; and he is no doubt acutely aware that Evangelicalism now dominates the Church.

The saga of Rowan's endorsements illustrates perfectly the ecclesiastical dilemma that this book seeks to address. When people of liberal persuasion, like me, still formed a substantial body within the Church, vigorous debate on all kinds of matters was commonplace; and the Church was comparatively vibrant. Of course, some anxious souls fretted that disagreements between Christians might give a bad impression to the wider world. But throughout the two millennia of its existence Christianity has tended to flourish when its internal debates have been lively.

But in becoming a one-party organization, which most liberal-minded people have withdrawn from or never join, the Church of England has lost its confidence, and become defensive and controlling. Diverse and dissenting views go largely unheard within its institutions, and the people holding them are regarded as an embarrassment – or, worse still, as disloyal. And as for the notion that individual parish churches should be set free, becoming open once again to all shades of belief and conviction, it is unthinkable.

The complaining Bishop is both right and wrong. To the great majority of the people outside the Church, the proposals contained in this book would seem rather mild, and amount to little more than common sense. Indeed, when the publisher first read the manuscript, he criticized me for not being sufficiently radical. Yet if the proposals in this book were taken seriously within the Church, they would, as the Bishop says, be explosive.

An acquaintance of mine, who is also a long-standing and close friend of Rowan's, said to me recently that he regards Rowan's appointment as the Church of England's 'last chance'. This acquaintance is devoted, as I am, to the parochial system, with its traditions of pastoral care and openness; and through his lifetime he has watched with horror as it has shrivelled. Although he is a layman, in his professional life he moves freely amongst the Church's bishops and senior clergy; and he is equally horrified by their lack of understanding of what is happening. Of course, the Church of England will survive, even if Rowan's tenure has little or no impact. But I agree that his leadership offers the last chance for the Church of England to begin re-establishing itself as the main spiritual home of the people of England.

If the saga of the disappearing endorsements holds any lessons, they are that Rowan Williams will have to resist the timidity of his colleagues, and not be deafened by the clamouring voices of the Evangelical establishment.